Practical Techniques for UI Designers

Crafting Intuitive Interfaces: Elevating User Interaction Design

writer name

DHAYANANDH RAVICHANDRAN

Table of Contents

WRITER'S NOTE

Hello, Dhayanandh Ravichandran here.

In today's fast-paced digital age, where users are inundated with countless apps, websites, and digital experiences vying for their attention, the significance of user interface design has never been more pronounced. User interfaces serve as the gateway to our digital world, shaping how we interact, engage, and ultimately perceive the services and products offered to us. Whether it's a seamless mobile app that simplifies daily tasks or a website that effortlessly guides us through complex information, intuitive interface design has become the cornerstone of crafting compelling user experiences. As technology continues to evolve and user expectations soar, the ability to create interfaces that are not just functional, but also intuitive and delightful, has emerged as a critical differentiator for businesses striving to stand out in a crowded digital landscape.

Importance of User Experience

User experience (UX) stands at the forefront of digital product success, serving as the linchpin that determines whether users will engage, return, and ultimately advocate for a product or service. At its core, UX encapsulates the entirety of an individual's interaction with a digital platform, encompassing not just the visual design, but also the functionality, usability, and emotional resonance of the experience.

In the fiercely competitive digital landscape, where alternatives are just a click away, user experience can make or break a product's viability. Studies have consistently shown a direct correlation between positive user experiences and key performance indicators such as customer satisfaction, retention rates, and even revenue growth. A seamless, intuitive user interface can transform an otherwise mundane task into a delightful experience, fostering a sense of loyalty and trust among users.

Intuitive interfaces play a pivotal role in enhancing user satisfaction and retention by streamlining interactions, minimizing cognitive load, and anticipating user needs. When users encounter interfaces that are intuitive and easy to navigate, they are more likely to feel empowered and in control, leading to higher levels of engagement and satisfaction. Moreover, intuitive interfaces instill a sense of confidence and competence in users, reducing the likelihood of frustration or abandonment.

In today's hyperconnected world, where users have come to expect seamless experiences across all digital touchpoints, businesses cannot afford to overlook the importance of user experience. By prioritizing intuitive interfaces and placing the needs of users at the forefront of design decisions, organizations can cultivate a loyal user base, drive sustainable growth, and position themselves for long-term success in an increasingly competitive landscape.

Understanding User Needs

In the realm of user interface design, one principle stands above all: understanding the needs and preferences of the end user. This foundational aspect cannot be overstated, as it forms the bedrock upon which intuitive and user-friendly interfaces are built. By delving into the intricacies of user behavior, preferences, and pain points, designers can tailor their creations to meet the specific needs of their target audience.

Intuitive UI design doesn't just happen by chance—it's a deliberate process rooted in empathy and user-centricity. By conducting thorough user research, which may involve techniques such as surveys, interviews, and usability testing, designers gain invaluable insights into user expectations and behavior. This deep understanding allows them to anticipate user needs, preempt potential pain points, and craft interfaces that feel intuitive and effortless to navigate.

Building Trust and Credibility

Trust and credibility are the cornerstones of any successful relationship, and the same holds true in the realm of user interface design. In today's digital landscape, where users are inundated with choices and scams abound, establishing trust is more important than ever. Intuitive interfaces play a pivotal role in this endeavor by fostering a sense of reliability, transparency, and authenticity.

Consider the sleek and intuitive interface of Apple's iPhone, which has garnered widespread acclaim for its user-friendly design. From its simple and elegant layout to its intuitive gestures and animations, every aspect of the iPhone's interface is meticulously crafted to instill confidence and trust in users. As a result, users feel comfortable and empowered to explore its features, knowing they are in capable hands.

Similarly, Google's search engine has become synonymous with intuitive design, thanks to its minimalist interface and lightning-fast performance. By prioritizing simplicity and clarity, Google has built a platform that users implicitly trust, making it their go-to destination for information retrieval.

These examples illustrate how intuitive interfaces can build trust and credibility with users, paving the way for long-lasting relationships and sustained success. By focusing on user needs, preferences, and expectations, designers can create interfaces that not only meet users' functional requirements but also resonate on a deeper, emotional level, earning their trust and loyalty in the process.

Increasing User Engagement

Intuitive interfaces are not only about making it easy for users to accomplish tasks but also about creating experiences that captivate and engage them. By removing barriers to interaction and providing seamless pathways to desired actions, intuitive interfaces play a crucial role in boosting user engagement and fostering deeper connections with digital products.

One key aspect of intuitive interfaces that contributes to increased user engagement is intuitive navigation. When users can effortlessly navigate through a digital platform, they are more likely to explore its features, discover new content, and spend more time interacting with it. Clear and concise messaging also plays a vital role in keeping users engaged by providing them with relevant information and guiding them through the user journey.

Responsive design is another essential component of intuitive interfaces that enhances user engagement. In today's multi-device landscape, where users access digital products across a variety of screens and devices, responsive design ensures a consistent and optimized experience regardless of the device used. By adapting seamlessly to different screen sizes and resolutions, responsive interfaces cater to the needs of users, allowing them to engage with the product on their preferred device without encountering any friction.

Reducing User Friction

User friction refers to any aspect of the user experience that impedes or frustrates users' ability to accomplish their goals. Intuitive UI design aims to minimize user friction by streamlining interactions, eliminating unnecessary steps, and anticipating user needs.

One common pain point for users is complex or convoluted navigation systems that make it difficult to find the information they're looking for. By implementing intuitive navigation structures, such as clear menus, breadcrumbs, and search functionality, designers can help users quickly locate the content they need without getting lost or frustrated.

Another source of user friction is unclear or confusing interface elements, such as ambiguous buttons or confusing terminology.

Intuitive UI design addresses this by using familiar conventions and language that users can easily understand and interpret. For example, using descriptive labels for buttons and actions helps users anticipate the outcome of their actions, reducing uncertainty and frustration.

By focusing on minimizing user friction and creating seamless, intuitive experiences, designers can create digital products that users enjoy using and are more likely to return to. Intuitive interfaces not only make it easier for users to accomplish their tasks but also contribute to overall satisfaction and loyalty.

Competitive Advantage

Intuitive interfaces offer more than just a pleasant user experience—they can serve as a powerful differentiator in today's competitive market landscape. Companies that prioritize intuitive design gain a significant advantage by setting themselves apart from competitors and capturing the attention of users. Intuitive interfaces not only attract new users but also retain existing ones, fostering loyalty and advocacy.

Consider the case of Airbnb, which revolutionized the hospitality industry by providing a user-friendly platform for booking accommodations worldwide. With its intuitive interface, streamlined search functionality, and personalized recommendations, Airbnb gained a competitive edge over traditional hotel booking services. By focusing on user needs and preferences, Airbnb created an experience that resonated with travelers, leading to rapid growth and market dominance.

Similarly, Slack emerged as a leader in the team collaboration space by offering a platform with an intuitive interface that simplifies communication and project management. By streamlining workflows and reducing friction in team interactions, Slack gained a loyal user base and surpassed competitors who struggled with clunky and unintuitive interfaces.

Impact on Business Goals

The impact of intuitive UI design extends beyond just enhancing the user experience—it directly influences key business goals such as conversion rates, user retention, and brand loyalty. Companies that invest in intuitive design see tangible results in terms of improved performance metrics and long-term sustainability.

Research consistently shows a strong correlation between intuitive design and business success. According to a study by the Nielsen Norman Group, every dollar invested in usability can result in a return on investment (ROI) of up to $100, highlighting the significant impact of intuitive design on business outcomes.

Intuitive interfaces contribute to higher conversion rates by guiding users seamlessly through the purchase journey and reducing friction in the checkout process. Additionally, intuitive design fosters user retention by creating positive experiences that encourage users to return to the platform and engage with it regularly.

Furthermore, intuitive interfaces play a crucial role in building brand loyalty and advocacy. When users have positive experiences with a product, they are more likely to recommend it to others and become loyal brand advocates. This not only leads to increased customer lifetime value but also reduces customer acquisition costs, providing a sustainable competitive advantage in the market.

By prioritizing intuitive UI design, companies can achieve their business goals more effectively and position themselves for long-term success in an increasingly competitive landscape.

Welcome to **"The Art of Intuitive Interfaces: Practical Techniques for UI Designers**." In this book, we'll embark on a journey to explore the principles, strategies, and techniques behind creating intuitive user interfaces that captivate and engage users. Each chapter is carefully crafted to provide you with actionable insights and practical tips that you can apply to your own design projects. Let's take a brief look at what each chapter has to offer:

1. **Fundamentals of UI Design:** We'll start by diving into the fundamentals of UI design, covering essential principles such as layout, typography, color theory, and visual hierarchy.

2. **User-Centered Design Approach:** Next, we'll explore the importance of understanding user needs and preferences, as well as techniques for conducting user research, creating personas, and iterating on designs based on user feedback.

3. **Responsive Design Principles:** In this chapter, we'll delve into the principles of responsive design and explore strategies for creating interfaces that adapt seamlessly to different screen sizes and devices.

4. **Accessibility in UI Design:** We'll discuss the importance of designing accessible interfaces that are usable by all users, regardless of their abilities, and explore techniques for ensuring accessibility in UI design.

5. **UI Patterns and Components:** Here, we'll explore common UI patterns and components, such as navigation menus, forms, and buttons, and discuss best practices for designing.

6. **Visual Design Techniques:** We'll dive into the details of visual design, including typography, imagery, and iconography, and explore how to create visually appealing interfaces that also communicate effectively.

7. **UI Animation for Engagement:** This chapter will explore the role of animation in UI design and provide practical tips for implementing animation effectively to enhance user engagement.

8. **Testing and Feedback:** We'll discuss the importance of testing UI designs with real users and gathering feedback to iterate and improve, covering various testing methods.

9. **Tools and Resources for UI Designers:** Finally, we'll provide an overview of the tools and resources available to

UI designers, including design software, prototyping tools, and online communities.

Delve into "The Art of Intuitive Interfaces" to uncover the secrets of UI design. Whether you're a seasoned pro or just starting out, this book offers invaluable insights. Learn the principles and techniques behind creating user-friendly interfaces that captivate and engage. With practical guidance and expert advice, you'll refine your skills and craft exceptional digital experiences. Explore each chapter to gain a deeper understanding of UI design fundamentals. Discover how to create intuitive layouts, choose the right typography, and use color effectively. Dive into the world of user-centered design and responsive interfaces. Whether you're designing websites or mobile apps, this book has you covered. Elevate your design skills and create interfaces that leave a lasting impression. Start your journey into the art and science of intuitive UI design today.

C H A P T E R O N E

Fundamentals of UI Design

> "
> Design is not just what it looks like and feels like. Design is
> how it works.

In today's digital age, user interface (UI) design plays a pivotal role in shaping the success of digital products and services. UI design serves as the bridge between users and technology, influencing how individuals interact, navigate, and engage with digital interfaces. From mobile apps to websites and software applications, the quality of UI design directly impacts user satisfaction, retention, and overall experience. Effective UI design goes beyond aesthetics; it encompasses principles of usability, accessibility, and visual communication to create interfaces that are intuitive, engaging, and delightful to use. In this chapter, we'll delve into the fundamentals of UI design, exploring key concepts such as layout, typography, color theory, and visual hierarchy. By mastering these fundamentals, designers can create compelling digital experiences that captivate users and drive success in today's competitive digital landscape.

Understanding layout

In the realm of UI design, the layout serves as the foundation upon which the entire user interface is built. It refers to the arrangement of visual elements within a digital interface, including text, images, buttons, and other interactive components. A well-designed layout is essential for creating a cohesive and organized user experience that guides users seamlessly through the interface.

The principles of balance, alignment, and white space are fundamental aspects of effective layout design. Balance ensures that visual elements are distributed evenly throughout the interface, creating a sense of harmony and stability. Alignment ensures that elements are placed in relation to each other in a way that creates visual coherence and clarity. White space, also known as negative space, refers to the empty areas between elements and plays a crucial role in enhancing readability, focus, and overall aesthetics.

There are various layout structures that designers can utilize, each with its own unique characteristics and advantages. Grid-based layouts, for example, are structured on a grid system, allowing for precise alignment and consistency across different screen sizes. Asymmetric layouts, on the other hand, embrace asymmetry and irregularity, creating dynamic and visually interesting compositions. Additionally, designers may also employ modular or hierarchical layouts, depending on the content and goals of the interface. By understanding the principles of layout design and experimenting with different structures, designers can create interfaces that are not only visually appealing but also functional and user-friendly.

Typography in UI Design

Typography plays a crucial role in user interface design, influencing both the readability of content and the overall visual appeal of the interface. Effective typography not only ensures that users can easily consume information but also contributes to the aesthetic quality and personality of the design. For instance, in a mobile application, choosing a legible font with appropriate spacing between characters can enhance readability, making it easier for users to navigate and interact with the app.

Understanding the basics of typography terminology is essential for UI designers. Font family refers to a group of typefaces with similar characteristics, such as serif, sans-serif, or monospaced. Each font family has its own distinct style and personality, which can evoke different emotions and perceptions. For example, a serif font like Times New Roman is often associated with tradition and formality, while a sans-serif font like Helvetica is perceived as modern and clean. Font size determines the overall size of the text and influences hierarchy and emphasis within the interface. Designers must consider factors such as legibility and screen size when choosing an appropriate font size. Font weight refers to the thickness or boldness of the characters, which can be used to create contrast and hierarchy within the typography.

Guidelines for choosing appropriate fonts for different contexts involve considering factors such as brand identity, target

audience, and intended message. For instance, a playful and informal font may be suitable for a children's educational app, while a more professional and sophisticated font may be preferable for a financial services website. Additionally, designers should ensure consistency in typography throughout the interface to maintain visual coherence and reinforce the brand identity. By understanding the principles of typography and applying them thoughtfully, designers can create interfaces that not only communicate effectively but also resonate with users on a visual and emotional level.

Color Theory

Color plays a fundamental role in user interface design, influencing user perception, emotion, and behavior. Understanding color psychology is essential for designers, as different colors can evoke specific feelings and associations in users. For example, warm colors like red and orange are often associated with energy, passion, and urgency, while cool colors like blue and green evoke feelings of calmness, trust, and stability. By leveraging the psychological effects of color, designers can create interfaces that resonate with users on a deeper level and evoke the desired emotional response

Color properties, including hue, saturation, and brightness, further contribute to the visual impact of a design. Hue refers to the actual color of an object, such as red, blue, or yellow. Saturation refers to the intensity or purity of a color, with highly saturated colors appearing vivid and vibrant, while desaturated

colors appear muted and subdued. Brightness, also known as value or lightness, refers to the relative lightness or darkness of a color. By manipulating these properties, designers can create color schemes that are visually appealing and harmonious.

Color harmonies, such as complementary, analogous, and triadic, offer guidelines for creating balanced and aesthetically pleasing color palettes in UI design. Complementary colors are opposite each other on the color wheel and create strong contrast when used together, making them ideal for highlighting important elements or creating visual interest. For example, a blue button on an orange background would stand out prominently. Analogous colors are adjacent to each other on the color wheel and create a harmonious and cohesive look when used together, such as a range of greens and blues in a nature-themed interface. Triadic colors are evenly spaced around the color wheel and offer a balanced combination of contrast and harmony, providing versatility in design compositions.

Create Imagination !!!

Imagine a fitness app that uses color psychology and harmonies to motivate and inspire users. The app's primary color scheme consists of vibrant shades of red and orange, evoking feelings of energy, excitement, and determination. The use of highly saturated colors conveys a sense of vitality and intensity, encouraging users to stay active and engaged. Additionally, the app incorporates complementary colors, such as blue accents for buttons and notifications, to provide visual contrast and draw attention to important actions. This combination of color psychology, properties, and harmonies creates a visually stimulating and emotionally uplifting user experience, motivating users to achieve their fitness goals.

Visual Hierarchy Principles

Visual hierarchy is the arrangement and presentation of elements within a design in a way that guides the user's attention and communicates the relative importance of each element. It plays a crucial role in helping users quickly understand and navigate through a user interface by organizing information in a clear and intuitive manner. Effective visual hierarchy ensures that users can easily identify key elements, such as headings, buttons, and calls to action, and prioritize their attention accordingly.

Designers employ various techniques to create visual hierarchy, leveraging factors such as size, color, contrast, and spacing. Size refers to the physical dimensions of elements within the interface, with larger elements typically drawing more attention than smaller ones. By strategically sizing elements based on their importance, designers can emphasize key elements and create a sense of hierarchy. For example, a larger headline will stand out more prominently than smaller body text, signaling its significance to the user.

Color is another powerful tool for establishing visual hierarchy, as different colors can convey different meanings and associations.

Bright, saturated colors tend to attract attention more than muted or desaturated colors, making them effective for highlighting important elements. Designers can use color strategically to draw attention to key elements, such as using a bold color for buttons or links to indicate interactivity.

Contrast plays a critical role in creating visual hierarchy by distinguishing between different elements within the interface. High-contrast combinations, such as black text on a white background, are easier to read and stand out more prominently than low-contrast combinations. By adjusting contrast between elements, designers can direct the user's attention and create a clear sense of hierarchy.

Spacing, or the distance between elements, also contributes to visual hierarchy by creating separation and organization within the interface. Adequate spacing between elements helps prevent visual clutter and allows users to easily distinguish between different elements. By adjusting spacing based on the importance of each element, designers can create a structured and visually appealing layout that guides the user's eye through the interface.

Examples of effective visual hierarchy in UI design can be found in various digital products and platforms.For instance, in an e-commerce website, the use of a large, bold headline followed by smaller product descriptions and pricing details creates a clear hierarchy that directs the user's attention from the most important information to secondary details.

Similarly, in a navigation menu, the use of color, size, and contrast to differentiate between primary and secondary menu items helps users quickly identify the most relevant options and navigate the site with ease. Overall, visual hierarchy is a powerful tool for designers to communicate information effectively and create user interfaces that are intuitive, engaging, and easy to use.

Case Study: Layout and Typography

Typography plays a significant role in enhancing the reading experience on Medium. The platform utilizes a serif font for body text, which is known for its readability in long-form content. The font size is carefully chosen to ensure comfortable reading on various screen sizes, while the line spacing provides ample room for the eyes to navigate between lines without feeling cramped. Additionally, Medium employs typography hierarchy to guide users through the content, with larger headings and subheadings indicating the structure and flow of the article.

he layout and typography choices on Medium contribute to a seamless and enjoyable reading experience for users. The clean and organized layout makes it easy for users to browse and discover new content, while the typography ensures that the text is legible and engaging. By prioritizing readability and user-centered design principles, Medium creates an environment where users can immerse themselves in quality content without distractions.

Overall, the thoughtful integration of layout and typography enhances the overall user experience on Medium and sets a high standard for digital publishing platforms.

Medium.com, a popular online publishing platform, provides an excellent example of effective layout structure and typography choices that contribute to the overall user experience. The layout of Medium's interface is clean, spacious, and organized, with a focus on readability and content consumption. Upon visiting the website, users are greeted with a simple yet elegant grid-based layout that presents a curated selection of articles in a visually appealing manner. The use of whitespace between articles creates a sense of balance and allows each piece of content to stand out independently.

Case Study: Color Theory in Action

Let's delve into the design of a fitness tracking app called "FitFuel" to understand how color theory principles are applied and how they influence user perception and interaction.

FitFuel employs a vibrant color scheme consisting of energetic shades of green, blue, and yellow, which aligns with the app's purpose of promoting health and wellness. These colors are carefully selected based on color psychology principles, with green representing vitality and growth, blue conveying trust and stability, and yellow evoking optimism and positivity. As users interact with the app, these colors subconsciously communicate messages of energy, reliability, and motivation, setting the tone for their fitness journey.

The application of color theory extends beyond aesthetics to enhance user interaction and usability. FitFuel utilizes color to differentiate between various elements within the interface, aiding users in navigation and comprehension. For instance, buttons and calls-to-action are prominently displayed in a contrasting color, such as bright yellow or orange, to draw users' attention and prompt them to take action, whether it's logging a workout or setting a new goal. Conversely, informational text and secondary elements are presented in softer hues or muted tones, ensuring that they do not compete for attention with more critical interface elements.

Furthermore, FitFuel leverages color harmony principles, such as complementary and analogous color schemes, to create visual harmony and cohesion throughout the app. Complementary colors, like green and magenta, are strategically used to create contrast and highlight important information, such as progress indicators or achievements. Analogous colors, such as shades of blue and teal, are employed for secondary elements, creating a sense of unity and flow within the interface.

Overall, the thoughtful application of color theory in FitFuel not only enhances the visual appeal of the app but also profoundly influences user perception and interaction. Through strategic color choices and harmonious combinations, FitFuel creates a dynamic and engaging user experience that motivates and empowers users on their fitness journey.

Case Study: Visual Hierarchy in Practice

Let's examine the design of a fictional e-commerce website called "Shopify" to illustrate effective use of visual hierarchy in practice. Shopify employs a well-crafted visual hierarchy to guide users through the interface and prioritize information effectively.

Upon landing on the homepage of Shopify, users are immediately drawn to the hero banner, which features high-quality product images and compelling call-to-action buttons, such as "Shop Now" or "Explore Deals." These elements are strategically positioned at the top of the page and presented in a larger size, bold font, and contrasting color to capture users' attention and encourage them to explore further.

As users scroll down the homepage, they encounter a series of product categories displayed in a grid layout. Each category is accompanied by a visually striking image and a concise heading, followed by a brief description or promotion. The use of larger font sizes for headings and prominent placement of images create visual emphasis, signaling the importance of these categories and enticing users to browse further.

Within each product category page, Shopify maintains a consistent visual hierarchy to facilitate easy navigation and decision-making. Product thumbnails are displayed in a grid format, with larger images and bold titles indicating featured or top-selling items. Users can quickly scan through the products and identify key details, such as price and ratings, thanks to clear typography and layout organization.

Throughout the interface, Shopify utilizes color, size, and spacing to establish a clear hierarchy of information. For example, pricing information is displayed in a larger font size or highlighted in a contrasting color to ensure visibility. Similarly, buttons for adding items to the cart or proceeding to checkout are designed with bold colors and ample spacing to make them stand out and encourage action.

Overall, Shopify's design effectively leads users through the interface by prioritizing information and guiding their attention to key elements. The thoughtful implementation of visual hierarchy ensures that users can navigate the website with ease, discover relevant products, and make informed purchasing decisions, ultimately contributing to a positive user experience.

Practical Tips for UI Designer

In summary, mastering the fundamentals of UI design, including layout, typography, color theory, and visual hierarchy, is essential for creating compelling and user-friendly interfaces. Here are some practical tips and best practices to keep in mind when applying these principles to your UI design projects:

1. **Prioritize Clarity and Simplicity:** Focus on creating layouts that are clean, organized, and easy to navigate. Avoid clutter and unnecessary elements that can overwhelm users and detract from the overall user experience.
2. Establish Consistency: Maintain consistency in layout, typography, color scheme, and visual style across your interface to create a cohesive and unified design. Consistency enhances usability and helps users understand and navigate the interface more effectively.
3. Use Hierarchy to Guide Attention: Utilize visual hierarchy techniques, such as size, color, and contrast, to prioritize

information and guide users' attention to key elements. Clearly distinguish between primary, secondary, and tertiary content to help users understand the structure and importance of the interface.

4. Optimize Typography for Readability: Choose legible fonts and appropriate font sizes for different types of content, ensuring that text is easy to read and understand. Pay attention to line spacing, line length, and text alignment to enhance readability and comfort for users.

5. Harness the Power of Color: Understand the psychological impact of color and use it strategically to evoke specific emotions and associations in users. Choose color schemes that complement your brand identity and reinforce the intended mood or message of your interface.

6. Test and Iterate: Continuously test your UI designs with real users to gather feedback and identify areas for improvement. Use usability testing, A/B testing, and analytics to measure user behavior and iteratively refine your designs based on user insights.

7. Stay Updated on Design Trends: Keep abreast of current design trends, best practices, and emerging technologies in UI design. Experiment with new techniques and tools to push the boundaries of your designs and stay ahead of the competition.

By incorporating these practical tips into your UI design process, you can create interfaces that are not only visually appealing but also intuitive, engaging, and user-centered. Remember that effective UI design is a blend of art and science, requiring creativity, empathy, and a deep understanding of user needs and behaviors.

Interactive Exercises

To reinforce the concepts learned in this chapter and hone your UI design skills, consider engaging in the following interactive exercises:

1. **Layout Redesign:** Choose a website or mobile app with a cluttered or poorly organized layout and redesign it to improve usability and visual appeal. Focus on simplifying the layout, optimizing spacing, and establishing clear visual hierarchy to guide users through the interface more effectively.

2. **Typography Exploration:** Experiment with different font pairings, sizes, and styles to create typographic compositions for various types of content, such as headlines, body text, and call-to-action buttons. Pay attention to readability, consistency, and aesthetic harmony as you explore different typography options.

3. **Color Palette Creation:** Create a color palette inspired by a specific theme or mood, such as nature, technology, or relaxation. Use color theory principles to select complementary or analogous colors that evoke the desired emotions and associations. Apply the color palette to a UI design project, such as a website or mobile app interface, and observe how it influences user perception and interaction.

4. **Visual Hierarchy Exercise:** Analyze existing UI designs or interfaces and identify examples of effective visual hierarchy. Study how elements such as size, color, contrast, and spacing are used to prioritize information and guide user attention. Then, apply these insights to your own design projects by creating wireframes or mockups that demonstrate clear visual hierarchy.

5. **Usability Testing:** Conduct usability testing sessions with friends, family, or colleagues to gather feedback on your UI design projects. Present users with specific tasks or scenarios to complete, such as finding a product or signing up for an account, and observe their interactions and feedback. Use the insights gained from usability testing to iterate and improve your designs iteratively.

These interactive exercises provide valuable opportunities to apply the concepts and techniques learned in this chapter in a hands-on manner. By actively engaging in these exercises, you can strengthen your UI design skills, deepen your understanding of design principles, and ultimately create better user experiences for your audience.

In conclusion, mastering the fundamentals of UI design is essential for creating engaging, intuitive, and user-friendly digital experiences. By understanding principles such as layout, typography, color theory, and visual hierarchy, designers can craft interfaces that not only look visually appealing but also function effectively and meet the needs of users. These fundamentals serve as the building blocks upon which successful UI design projects are built, providing a solid foundation for creativity, innovation, and problem-solving. As you continue on your UI design journey, I encourage you to explore and practice these fundamentals regularly, seeking opportunities to refine your skills and expand your knowledge. Whether you're a seasoned designer or just starting out, there's always something new to learn and discover in the dynamic and ever-evolving field of UI design. Embrace the challenge, stay curious, and never stop learning as you strive to create meaningful and impactful digital experiences for your audience.

C H A P T E R T W O

User Centered Design Approach

❝

The details are not the details. They make the design.

User-centered design (UCD) is an iterative design process in which the needs, preferences, and behaviors of end-users are given primary consideration at each stage of the product development lifecycle. The goal of UCD is to create products and services that are intuitive, efficient, and satisfying for users by involving them in the design process from the outset. In this chapter, we'll explore the key principles and methodologies of UCD, including user research methods, creating user personas and journey mapping, and prototyping with iterative design.

Understanding User Research Methods

User research is the foundation of UCD, providing valuable insights into the needs, motivations, and behaviors of target users. Various research methods can be employed to gather qualitative and quantitative data, such as interviews, surveys, observation, and usability testing. Each method offers unique advantages and challenges, and the choice of research methods should be tailored to the specific goals and constraints of the project. By conducting user research early and often, designers can gain a deep understanding of user needs and preferences, informing design decisions throughout the product development process.

Creating User Personas

Creating user personas is a pivotal step in the user-centered design process, as it enables designers to humanize their target audience and develop a deeper understanding of their needs, goals, and behaviors. User personas are fictional representations of archetypal users, crafted based on insights gleaned from user research and data analysis. Each persona typically includes demographic information, such as age, gender, occupation, and location, as well as psychographic details, such as motivations, pain points, and behavioral tendencies. By synthesizing user data into personas, designers can gain valuable insights into the diverse needs and preferences of their target audience, allowing them to design products and services that resonate with real users. Additionally, user personas serve as invaluable tools for aligning stakeholders around user-centric design decisions, fostering empathy and understanding across multidisciplinary teams. In the following sections, we will explore the process of creating user personas in greater detail, examining best practices, common pitfalls, and practical applications in real-world design projects.

Journey Mapping

Journey mapping is a powerful technique that allows designers to visualize and understand the end-to-end user experience across various touchpoints and interactions. By mapping out the user journey, from initial discovery to post-interaction follow-up, designers can gain valuable insights into the emotions, motivations, and pain points that users experience at each stage of their interaction with a product or service. Journey maps typically consist of a series of chronological steps or stages, accompanied by detailed descriptions of user actions, thoughts, and feelings at each touchpoint.

Moreover, journey mapping provides designers with a holistic view of the user experience, enabling them to identify opportunities for improvement, optimization, and innovation. By pinpointing key moments of delight or frustration along the user journey, designers can prioritize design efforts and allocate resources more effectively to address critical pain points and enhance positive interactions. Additionally, journey maps serve as valuable communication tools for aligning stakeholders around user-centric design decisions and fostering cross-functional collaboration across teams.

In practice, journey mapping can take various forms, ranging from simple diagrams or flowcharts to more elaborate visualizations that incorporate multimedia elements, such as photos, videos, or quotes from user interviews. Regardless of the format, the primary goal of journey mapping remains the same: to cultivate empathy and understanding for the end user, ultimately leading to the creation of more intuitive, empathetic, and user-centered products and services. In the following sections, we will delve deeper into the process of journey mapping, exploring best practices, common pitfalls, and real-world applications in the field of user-centered design.

Prototyping and Iterative Design

Prototyping and iterative design are integral components of the user-centered design process, enabling designers to test, refine, and improve their designs based on user feedback and insights. Prototyping involves creating tangible representations of design concepts, ranging from low-fidelity wireframes to high-fidelity interactive prototypes, that simulate the functionality and user experience of the final product. These prototypes serve as valuable tools for validating design assumptions, exploring different design solutions, and gathering feedback from stakeholders and end users.

One of the key benefits of prototyping is its ability to facilitate rapid experimentation and iteration. Designers can quickly create multiple iterations of a design, incorporating feedback and making improvements based on user testing and evaluation. This iterative approach allows designers to identify and address usability issues, refine interactions, and optimize the overall user experience over time. By testing early and often with real users, designers can validate design decisions, mitigate risks, and ultimately create products that better meet the needs and expectations of their target audience.

Moreover, prototyping fosters collaboration and communication among multidisciplinary teams, enabling designers, developers, and stakeholders to align around a shared vision and iterate on design solutions collaboratively. By creating tangible prototypes that stakeholders can interact with and provide feedback on, designers can bridge the gap between conceptual ideas and tangible outcomes, facilitating more informed and effective decision-making throughout the design process.

In summary, prototyping and iterative design play a crucial role in the user-centered design process, empowering designers to create more user-centric, intuitive, and impactful products and services. By prototyping early and iterating often, designers can refine their designs based on user feedback, validate design decisions, and ultimately deliver superior user experiences that resonate with their target audience. In the following sections, we will explore best practices, tools, and techniques for prototyping and iterative design, as well as real-world examples of their application in the field of user-centered design.

Conclusion and Practical Application

In conclusion, the user-centered design approach places users at the heart of the design process, ensuring that products and services are tailored to their needs, preferences, and behaviors. By employing user research methods, creating user personas and journey mapping, and prototyping with iterative design, designers can create more intuitive, efficient, and satisfying user experiences.

C HAPTER T HREE

Responsive Design Principles

User interface is like a joke. If you have to explain it, it's

not that good

In today's digital landscape, where users access websites and applications across a myriad of devices with varying screen sizes and resolutions, the need for responsive design has never been more critical. Responsive design represents a paradigm shift in web development, aiming to provide users with a consistent and optimized experience regardless of the device they're using. At its core, responsive design is driven by the philosophy of adaptability and flexibility, ensuring that websites and applications can seamlessly adjust and respond to the unique characteristics of each user's device.

Responsive design encompasses a range of techniques and principles aimed at creating layouts and interfaces that are fluid, flexible, and adaptable to different screen sizes and resolutions. One of the fundamental aspects of responsive design is the use of fluid grids, which enable the layout of a website to expand and contract dynamically based on the dimensions of the user's viewport. By using relative units such as percentages instead of fixed units like pixels, fluid grids ensure that content can be displayed proportionally across devices, maintaining visual harmony and readability.

In addition to fluid grids, responsive design relies on flexible images and media queries to optimize the presentation of content across different devices. Flexible images scale proportionally based on the size of the viewport, preventing images from becoming distorted or overflowing on smaller screens. Media queries, on the other hand, allow designers to apply different styles and layouts based on the characteristics of the user's device, such as screen width, height, and orientation. By using media queries, designers can create breakpoints at which the layout of the website adjusts to accommodate different screen sizes and device types, ensuring a seamless and optimized experience for users.

Responsive design is not just about making websites look good on mobile devices; it's about creating experiences that are accessible, usable, and engaging across all devices and screen sizes. By adopting a responsive design approach, designers can future-proof their websites and applications, ensuring that they remain relevant and effective in an increasingly mobile-centric world. In the following sections, we will explore the principles, strategies, and best practices of responsive design in greater detail, equipping you with the knowledge and tools to create responsive interfaces that delight and empower users.

Basics of Responsive Design

Responsive design is a foundational concept in modern web development, aimed at ensuring that websites and applications can adapt and respond seamlessly to the diverse array of devices and screen sizes used by today's users. At its core, responsive design revolves around the principles of flexibility, adaptability, and user-centricity, with the ultimate goal of delivering an optimal user experience across all devices.

1. **Fluid Grids**

   One of the fundamental aspects of responsive design is the use of fluid grids. Unlike traditional fixed-width layouts, which are designed to display content at specific pixel dimensions, fluid grids allow the layout of a website to adjust dynamically based on the dimensions of the user's viewport. This is achieved by using relative units such as percentages instead of fixed units like pixels to define the width and positioning of elements within the layout.

   The key advantage of fluid grids is their ability to scale proportionally to fit different screen sizes and resolutions, ensuring that content remains visually appealing and accessible across a wide range of devices. Whether viewed on a desktop monitor, a tablet, or a smartphone, websites built with fluid grids can adapt to the available screen real estate, providing users with a consistent and optimized experience.

2. **Flexible Images**

In addition to fluid grids, responsive design relies on flexible images to ensure that visual content remains accessible and visually appealing across devices

Flexible images scale proportionally based on the size of the viewport, preventing them from becoming distorted or overflowing on smaller screens. This is achieved by specifying the dimensions of images using relative units such as percentages or the max-width property in CSS.

By using flexible images, designers can ensure that visual content, such as photographs, illustrations, and icons, adapts seamlessly to different screen sizes and resolutions. This not only enhances the visual appeal of websites and applications but also improves usability by ensuring that users can access and interact with visual content regardless of the device they're using.

3. **Media Queries**

Media queries are CSS rules that allow designers to apply different styles and layouts based on the characteristics of the user's device, such as screen width, height, and orientation. By using media queries, designers can create breakpoints at which the layout of the website adjusts to accommodate different screen sizes and device types, ensuring a seamless and optimized experience for users.

Media queries are commonly used to define specific styles for different device categories, such as desktops, tablets, and smartphones, as well as to implement responsive design patterns, such as hiding or rearranging content based on the available screen real estate.

By leveraging media queries, designers can create flexible and adaptable layouts that provide users with a consistent and optimized experience across all devices.

In summary, the basics of responsive design revolve around the principles of fluid grids, flexible images, and media queries. By embracing these concepts, designers can create websites and applications that adapt and respond seamlessly to the diverse array of devices and screen sizes used by today's users, ensuring a consistent and optimized user experience across all platforms.

Strategies for Mobile-First Design

Mobile-first design is a design approach that prioritizes the development of the mobile version of a website or application before scaling up to larger screen sizes. This strategy recognizes the increasing prevalence of mobile devices as the primary means of accessing the internet and the importance of delivering a fast, efficient, and user-friendly experience on smaller screens.

One of the key strategies for mobile-first design is content prioritization. This involves identifying and prioritizing the most critical content and features for the mobile experience, ensuring that users can access essential information quickly and easily, even on small screens. By focusing on the core functionality and content that users need most frequently, designers can create streamlined and efficient mobile experiences that prioritize usability and convenience.

Another strategy for mobile-first design is progressive enhancement. This approach involves starting with a basic, functional design that works across all devices and then layering on additional features and enhancements for larger screens. By designing for mobile devices first, designers can ensure that the core functionality of the website or application is accessible to all users, regardless of their device or screen size. As screen real estate increases, designers can then enhance the user experience with additional features, richer interactions, and more elaborate layouts, providing users with a more immersive and engaging experience on larger screens.

Additionally, mobile-first design encourages designers to embrace simplicity and minimalism in their designs. Given the limited screen space available on mobile devices, designers must prioritize clarity, simplicity, and efficiency in their designs, avoiding clutter and unnecessary elements that can overwhelm users and detract from the user experience. By focusing on essential content and functionality, designers can create mobile experiences that are intuitive, easy to navigate, and visually appealing.

Furthermore, mobile-first design emphasizes performance optimization and load time considerations. With mobile devices often operating on slower network connections and less powerful hardware than desktop computers, designers must performance and optimize their designs for speed and efficiency. This includes optimizing images and multimedia content, minimizing HTTP requests, and leveraging techniques such as lazy loading and code splitting to reduce load times and improve overall performance.

In summary, mobile-first design is not just about designing for smaller screens; it's about adopting a mindset that prioritizes the needs and preferences of mobile users from the outset. By embracing content prioritization, progressive enhancement, simplicity, and performance optimization, designers can create mobile experiences that are fast, efficient, and user-friendly, providing users with a seamless and enjoyable experience across all devices.

In conclusion, the principles and strategies outlined in this chapter underscore the importance of adopting a user-centric approach to web design, particularly in the context of responsive and mobile-first design. By prioritizing the needs and preferences of users across devices, designers can create experiences that are not only visually appealing but also intuitive, efficient, and engaging.

Moving forward, it's essential for designers to embrace these principles and integrate them into their design processes. This involves conducting thorough user research to understand the diverse needs and behaviors of users, creating user personas and journey maps to inform design decisions, and employing responsive design techniques to ensure that websites and applications adapt seamlessly to different screen sizes and devices.

Furthermore, designers should prioritize mobile-first design principles to create experiences that are optimized for mobile devices and provide users with a fast, efficient, and user-friendly experience on smaller screens. This involves prioritizing content, embracing simplicity and minimalism, and optimizing performance to ensure that mobile users can access essential information quickly and easily.

In practical terms, designers can begin by incorporating these principles and strategies into their design workflows, conducting regular usability testing and iteration to gather feedback and refine designs based on user insights. Additionally, designers should stay informed about emerging trends and best practices in responsive and mobile-first design, continuously learning and adapting to meet the evolving needs of users and technology.

Ultimately, by adopting a user-centric approach and embracing responsive and mobile-first design principles, designers can create experiences that resonate with users, foster engagement and loyalty, and drive business success. Whether designing websites, applications, or digital products, the ultimate goal should always be to create experiences that delight and empower users, regardless of the device they're using.

CHAPTER FOUR

Accessibility in UI Design

> ❝❝
>
> In UX, the conclusion marks the journey's fulfillment,
>
> leaving lasting impressions.

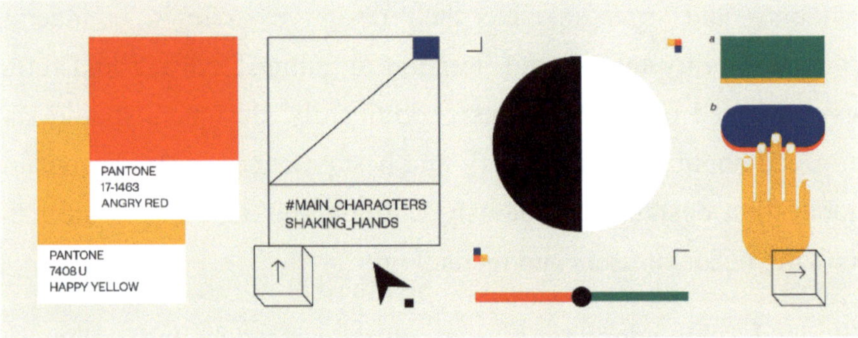

Accessibility in user interface (UI) design has emerged as a crucial consideration in today's digital landscape. It revolves around the principle of ensuring that digital products and interfaces are usable by everyone, regardless of their abilities or disabilities. With an increasing reliance on technology in all aspects of life, the importance of accessibility cannot be overstated. It's not just about compliance with regulations; it's about creating inclusive experiences that empower all users to access information, engage with content, and interact with interfaces effectively.

At its core, accessibility encompasses a broad spectrum of considerations, ranging from physical impairments to cognitive and situational limitations. Designing for accessibility involves understanding and addressing the diverse needs and preferences of users, including those with visual, auditory, motor, cognitive, or neurological impairments. It also extends to temporary disabilities, such as a broken arm or temporary vision loss, as well as situational limitations, such as using a device in bright sunlight or in a noisy environment.

The concept of accessibility is deeply rooted in the principles of equality, diversity, and inclusivity. It is a fundamental human right that ensures that everyone, regardless of their abilities or disabilities, has equal access to information, services, and opportunities. By designing accessible interfaces, designers not only comply with legal requirements but also uphold ethical and moral responsibilities to create a more inclusive and equitable digital environment.

In this chapter, we will explore the principles, strategies, and practical techniques for designing accessible user interfaces. We will delve into the key considerations and best practices for creating interfaces that are perceivable, operable, understandable, and robust for all users. From providing alternative text for images to ensuring keyboard accessibility and color contrast, we will cover a range of techniques aimed at improving usability and inclusivity for diverse user groups.

Ultimately, the goal of designing for accessibility is to break down barriers and create experiences that are inclusive, user-friendly, and empowering for everyone. By prioritizing accessibility in UI design, designers can play a pivotal role in fostering a more inclusive digital future, where everyone has equal access to information and opportunities, regardless of their abilities or disabilities.

Understanding User Needs

In the realm of accessibility-focused UI design, a profound understanding of user needs serves as the cornerstone for creating interfaces that are not only usable but also inclusive and empowering. User needs encompass a broad spectrum of requirements, preferences, and challenges that individuals may encounter when interacting with digital products and interfaces. It's essential for designers to adopt a user-centric approach, empathizing with users and gaining insights into their diverse experiences and perspectives.

User research lies at the heart of understanding user needs. Through methods such as interviews, surveys, observations, and usability testing, designers can gather invaluable insights into the capabilities, limitations, and preferences of their target audience. By engaging directly with users, designers can gain a deeper understanding of their needs, motivations, and pain points, allowing them to tailor interfaces to better meet user expectations.

Moreover, it's crucial for designers to recognize the diverse range of users who may interact with their interfaces. This includes individuals with visual impairments, auditory impairments, motor impairments, cognitive impairments, and neurological conditions, as well as those with temporary disabilities or situational limitations. Each user group has unique needs and preferences, and it's essential for designers to consider these factors when designing accessible interfaces.

Empathy plays a pivotal role in understanding user needs. By putting themselves in the shoes of users and experiencing interfaces from their perspective, designers can gain valuable insights into the challenges and barriers that users may encounter. This empathy-driven approach allows designers to identify opportunities for improvement and innovation, leading to interfaces that are more inclusive and user-friendly.

In addition to direct user research, designers can leverage existing resources and guidelines to better understand user needs. Resources such as the Web Content Accessibility Guidelines (WCAG) provide comprehensive guidance on creating accessible interfaces, covering topics such as perceivability, operability, understandability, and robustness. By familiarizing themselves with these guidelines, designers can ensure that their interfaces meet the needs of a diverse range of users.

Ultimately, understanding user needs is not a one-time endeavor but an ongoing process that evolves with the needs and preferences of users. By adopting a user-centric approach, engaging directly with users, and leveraging resources and guidelines, designers can create interfaces that are not only accessible but also inclusive and empowering for all users. In the following sections, we will delve deeper into the principles and techniques for designing accessible interfaces, equipping designers with the knowledge and tools to create interfaces that meet the diverse needs of their users.

Key Principles of Accessible Design

Accessible design is guided by several key principles that aim to ensure usability and inclusivity for all users, regardless of their abilities or disabilities. These principles serve as foundational pillars for creating interfaces that are perceivable, operable, understandable, and robust, thereby providing a seamless and empowering experience for all users.

1. **Perceivable**

   The principle of perceivability emphasizes the importance of presenting information and user interface components in a way that is perceivable to all users, including those with visual or auditory impairments. This involves providing alternative formats for content, such as alternative text for images, captions for videos, and descriptive headings for navigation. By ensuring that content is accessible to users with different sensory abilities, designers can create interfaces that are inclusive and equitable for all users.

2. **Operable**

   The operability principle focuses on ensuring that interfaces are operable by users of all abilities, including those with motor or dexterity impairments. This involves providing multiple ways for users to interact with the interface, such as keyboard shortcuts, voice commands, and gesture-based inputs. Additionally, interfaces should be designed with sufficient clickable area for interactive elements, ensuring that users can easily navigate and interact with the interface using a variety of input methods.

3. Understandable

The principle of understandability emphasizes the importance of designing interfaces in a way that is understandable to all users, including those with cognitive or language barriers. This involves using clear and concise language, organizing content logically, and providing instructions or cues to guide users through tasks. By designing interfaces that are easy to understand and navigate, designers can empower users to access information and perform tasks with confidence and independence.

4. Robust

The robustness principle focuses on ensuring that interfaces are robust enough to be interpreted reliably by a wide range of assistive technologies and devices. This involves following web standards and best practices for markup, ensuring compatibility with screen readers and other assistive technologies, and testing designs across different platforms and devices. By creating interfaces that are interoperable and compatible with assistive technologies, designers can ensure that all users can access and interact with the interface effectively.

By adhering to these key principles of accessible design, designers can create interfaces that are inclusive, usable, and empowering for all users, regardless of their abilities or disabilities. In the following sections, we will explore practical techniques and best practices for implementing these principles in UI design, equipping designers with the knowledge and tools to create accessible interfaces that meet the diverse needs of their users.

Practical Techniques for Accessible Design

Implementing accessible design involves a combination of technical considerations, design best practices, and empathy for users with diverse needs. Here are some practical techniques and strategies for creating accessible user interfaces:

1. **Providing Alternative Text for Images**

Alternative text, also known as alt text, is a brief description of an image that is read aloud by screen readers for users who are visually impaired. By providing descriptive alt text for images, designers ensure that users with visual impairments can access the content and context conveyed by images on the interface.

2. **Using Semantic HTML**

Semantic HTML elements provide meaning and structure to content, making it easier for screen readers and other assistive technologies to interpret and navigate. By using semantic elements such as headings, lists, and landmarks, designers can create interfaces that are more accessible and navigable for users with disabilities.

3. Ensuring Sufficient Color Contrast

High color contrast between text and background elements improves readability for users with visual impairments or color vision deficiencies. Designers should ensure that text meets minimum contrast ratios specified by accessibility guidelines, making it easier for all users to read and understand content.

4. Implementing Keyboard Accessibility

Keyboard accessibility is essential for users who cannot use a mouse or other pointing device due to motor impairments or other disabilities. Designers should ensure that all interactive elements, such as links, buttons, and form fields, can be accessed and activated using keyboard navigation alone.

5. Designing for Scalability and Flexibility

Interfaces should be designed to adapt to different screen sizes, resolutions, and zoom levels, ensuring usability for users with low vision or other visual impairments. Designers should use responsive design techniques to create layouts that are fluid and flexible, accommodating a wide range of devices and viewport sizes.

6. Providing Clear and Consistent Navigation

Clear and consistent navigation structures help users understand the layout of the interface and find the information they need more easily. Designers should use descriptive labels, logical grouping, and predictable navigation patterns to create interfaces that are intuitive and easy to navigate for all users.

7. Testing with Assistive Technologies

Testing with assistive technologies such as screen readers, magnification software, and voice recognition tools is essential for ensuring the accessibility of an interface. Designers should conduct regular accessibility audits and usability tests with users who have disabilities to identify and address accessibility barriers effectively.

8. Incorporating User Feedback

User feedback is invaluable for identifying accessibility issues and improving the usability of an interface. Designers should actively seek feedback from users with disabilities and incorporate their input into the design process to create interfaces that better meet their needs and preferences.

By incorporating these practical techniques into their design process, designers can create interfaces that are not only accessible but also more usable and inclusive for all users. Accessibility should be considered from the outset of the design process and integrated into every stage of development, from wireframing and prototyping to final implementation and testing. By prioritizing accessibility in UI design, designers can create interfaces that empower all users to access information, engage with content, and interact with interfaces effectively, regardless of their abilities or disabilities.

C H A P T E R F I V E

UI Patterns and Components

In UI design, patterns and components form the building blocks of user experiences.

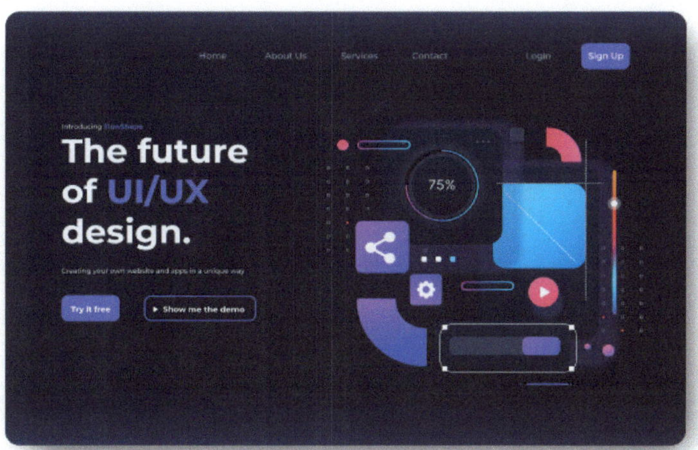

User Interface (UI) patterns and components play a crucial role in the design and development of digital products, providing designers and developers with reusable solutions to common design problems and interface challenges. UI patterns are recurring solutions to design problems that have been proven to be effective and efficient, while UI components are modular elements that can be combined and customized to create interfaces that are both visually appealing and functional. In this chapter, we will explore a variety of UI patterns and components, discussing their characteristics, use cases, and best practices for implementation.

The Significance of UI Patterns

UI patterns are foundational elements of UI design, offering a systematic approach to solving design problems and improving usability. They represent established solutions to recurring design challenges, distilled from years of design experience and user feedback. By leveraging UI patterns, designers can streamline the design process, reduce cognitive load for users, and create interfaces that are consistent and familiar.

Furthermore, UI patterns play a crucial role in enhancing the user experience by providing users with intuitive and predictable interactions. When users encounter familiar patterns in an interface, they can quickly understand how to navigate and interact with the interface, leading to a smoother and more enjoyable user experience. Additionally, UI patterns help establish visual hierarchy, guide users' attention, and communicate the underlying structure of the interface, further enhancing usability and clarity.

Characteristics of UI Patterns

UI patterns exhibit several key characteristics that distinguish them from ad-hoc design solutions. These characteristics include:

1. **Reusability**

   UI patterns are designed to be reusable across different projects and contexts. Once established, a pattern can be applied to various parts of an interface or even across different interfaces, saving time and effort for designers and ensuring consistency and coherence in the design.

2. **Consistency**

UI patterns promote consistency in design by providing a standard solution to a particular design problem. By using consistent patterns throughout an interface, designers can create a cohesive and unified user experience, making it easier for users to understand and navigate the interface.

3. **Predictability**

   UI patterns are familiar to users, making interactions more predictable and intuitive. When users encounter a familiar pattern in an interface, they can anticipate how it will behave and what actions are possible, reducing uncertainty and cognitive effort.

4. **Flexibility**

While UI patterns provide a standardized solution to a design problem, they also allow for flexibility and customization. Designers can adapt and modify patterns to fit the specific context and requirements of their project, ensuring that the design meets the needs of the target audience.

Applications of UI Patterns

UI patterns find application across a wide range of design contexts and interfaces, from websites and mobile apps to desktop software and interactive kiosks. Some common applications of UI patterns include:

1. **Navigation Patterns**

Navigation patterns help users find their way around an interface, providing intuitive ways to access content and navigate between different sections. Examples include top navigation bars, sidebars, breadcrumbs, and tabbed interfaces.

2. **Form Patterns**

Form patterns assist users in inputting and submitting information effectively, ensuring that the form is easy to understand and complete. Examples include single-column forms, multi-step forms, and inline validation.

3. Content Display Patterns

Content display patterns help organize and present content in a visually appealing and digestible format. Examples include card-based layouts, grid layouts, and list views.

In summary, UI patterns are fundamental elements of UI design, providing designers with reusable solutions to common design problems and interaction challenges. By leveraging UI patterns, designers can streamline the design process, improve usability, and create interfaces that are intuitive, efficient, and user-friendly.

Common UI Patterns

User Interface (UI) patterns are recurring solutions to design problems that have been proven to be effective and efficient. These patterns help designers create interfaces that are intuitive, consistent, and familiar to users. In this section, we will explore some of the most common UI patterns used in digital design, discussing their characteristics, use cases, and best practices for implementation.

1. Form Patterns

Form patterns assist users in inputting and submitting information effectively, ensuring that the form is easy to understand and complete. Examples include single-column forms, multi-step forms, and inline validation.

2. Content Display Patterns

Content display patterns help organize and present content in a visually appealing and digestible format. Examples include card-based layouts, grid layouts, and list views.

In summary, UI patterns are fundamental elements of UI design, providing designers with reusable solutions to common design problems and interaction challenges. By leveraging UI patterns, designers can streamline the design process, improve usability, and create interfaces that are intuitive, efficient, and user-friendly.

Common UI Patterns

User Interface (UI) patterns are recurring solutions to design problems that have been proven to be effective and efficient. These patterns help designers create interfaces that are intuitive, consistent, and familiar to users. In this section, we will explore some of the most common UI patterns used in digital design, discussing their characteristics, use cases, and best practices for implementation.

Navigation Patterns

Navigation patterns are essential for helping users find their way around a website or application. They provide intuitive ways to access content and navigate between different sections of the interface. Some common navigation patterns include:

1. Top Navigation Bar

A top navigation bar is a horizontal menu located at the top of the interface, typically containing links to the main sections or pages of the website. This pattern is ideal for websites with a small to medium number of pages.

2. Sidebar Navigation

Sidebar navigation consists of a vertical menu located on the side of the interface, typically used for accessing secondary or nested sections of the website. This pattern is suitable for websites with a large number of pages or hierarchical content.

3. Breadcrumb Navigation

Breadcrumb navigation displays the user's current location within the website's hierarchy, making it easier for users to understand their position and navigate back to previous pages. This pattern is especially useful for websites with deep hierarchies or complex navigation paths.

4. Tabbed Interface

A tabbed interface organizes content into tabs, allowing users to switch between different sections or views of the interface. This pattern is commonly used for organizing content into categories or providing multiple views of the same data.

Form Patterns

Forms are a common feature of many digital interfaces, allowing users to input and submit information. Form patterns help designers create forms that are easy to understand and complete. Some common form patterns include:

1. **Single-Column Form**

A single-column form arranges form fields in a single column, making it easy for users to scan and complete the form. This pattern is ideal for forms with a small to medium number of fields.

2. **Multi-Step Form**

A multi-step form breaks a longer form into multiple steps or pages, guiding users through the form one section at a time. This pattern helps prevent form fatigue and improves completion rates, especially for longer or more complex forms.

3. **Inline Validation**

Inline validation provides real-time feedback to users as they fill out a form, helping them correct errors and submit the form successfully. This pattern improves the user experience by reducing frustration and streamlining the form submission process.

4. Input Masks

Input masks format user input as they type, making it easier for users to enter information in a specific format (e.g., phone numbers, dates, credit card numbers). This pattern helps prevent formatting errors and improves data accuracy.

Content Display Patterns

Content display patterns help designers organize and present content in a visually appealing and digestible format. These patterns are essential for creating interfaces that are engaging and easy to navigate. Some common content display patterns include:

1. Card-Based Layout

A card-based layout organizes content into cards, each containing a piece of information or a visual element. This pattern is popular for displaying a variety of content types, such as articles, products, and images, in a visually appealing and modular format.

2. Grid Layout

A grid layout arranges content into a grid of evenly spaced rows and columns, making it easy for users to scan and compare items. This pattern is commonly used for displaying collections of items, such as product listings or image galleries.

3. List View

A list view presents content in a linear list format, with each item displayed sequentially. This pattern is ideal for displaying a large number of items in a compact space, such as search results or navigation menus.

In conclusion, these common UI patterns serve as foundational elements of digital design, providing designers with reusable solutions to common design problems and interaction challenges. By leveraging these patterns, designers can create interfaces that are intuitive, consistent, and engaging for users. However, it's essential for designers to use patterns thoughtfully and appropriately, considering the specific needs and preferences of their target audience and customizing patterns to fit the unique context and requirements of their project. With careful planning and execution, designers can create interfaces that deliver a seamless and enjoyable user experience.

Best Practices for Using UI Patterns

While UI patterns offer numerous benefits in terms of efficiency and usability, it's essential for designers to employ them thoughtfully and strategically. Here are some best practices for using UI patterns effectively in digital design:

Before incorporating UI patterns into a design, it's crucial to thoroughly understand the needs and preferences of the target audience. Consider factors such as demographics, device preferences, and user goals to ensure that the chosen patterns align with user expectations and behavior. Additionally, consider the context in which the interface will be used, such as the user's environment and the specific tasks they need to accomplish. By understanding the user's context, designers can choose patterns that enhance usability and improve the overall user experience.

Maintain Consistency Across the Interface

Consistency is key to creating a cohesive and intuitive user experience. When using UI patterns, strive to maintain consistency across different parts of the interface, such as navigation menus, form layouts, and content display patterns. Use the same patterns and components wherever possible to create a familiar and predictable experience for users. Consistency not only improves usability but also helps reinforce the brand identity and visual language of the interface.

Customize Patterns to Fit the Context

While UI patterns provide a standardized solution to a design problem, they should be customized and adapted to fit the specific context and requirements of the project. Avoid using patterns blindly and instead tailor them to the unique needs and goals of the interface. Consider factors such as branding, content structure, and user preferences when customizing patterns to ensure that they align with the overall design vision and objectives.

Test and Iterate

Usability testing is essential for evaluating the effectiveness of UI patterns and identifying areas for improvement. Conduct regular usability tests with real users to gather feedback and iterate on the design, making adjustments as needed to optimize the user experience. Pay attention to how users interact with the interface, identify pain points and usability issues, and use the insights gained from testing to refine and enhance the design. By testing and iterating on the design, designers can ensure that the chosen patterns are effective and well-suited to the needs of the target audience.

Consider Accessibility and Inclusivity

Accessibility should be a primary consideration when selecting and implementing UI patterns. Ensure that the chosen patterns are accessible to users with disabilities, such as visual impairments, motor impairments, and cognitive impairments. Use accessible design principles and guidelines, such as the Web Content Accessibility Guidelines (WCAG), to ensure that the interface is perceivable, operable, understandable, and robust for all users. By designing with accessibility in mind, designers can create interfaces that are inclusive and accessible to a diverse range of users.

In conclusion, using UI patterns effectively requires careful consideration of user needs, context, and accessibility, as well as a commitment to maintaining consistency and usability across the interface. By following best practices and customizing patterns to fit the unique requirements of the project, designers can create interfaces that are intuitive, engaging, and accessible to users.

Introduction to UI Components

In the realm of user interface (UI) design, UI components are the building blocks that form the visual and interactive elements of digital interfaces. These components encompass a wide range of elements, including buttons, input fields, sliders, cards, and navigation bars, among others. UI components play a vital role in creating interfaces that are not only visually appealing but also functional, intuitive, and consistent.

Significance of UI Components

UI components serve as the foundational elements of UI design, providing designers with reusable solutions to common design problems and interaction challenges. By leveraging UI components, designers can streamline the design process, reduce development time, and ensure consistency across different parts of the interface. Additionally, UI components contribute to the overall user experience by providing intuitive and familiar interactions that users can quickly understand and navigate.

UI components also play a crucial role in establishing the visual language and branding of an interface. Consistent use of UI components helps reinforce the brand identity and visual hierarchy of the interface, creating a cohesive and unified user experience. Furthermore, UI components contribute to the accessibility and inclusivity of an interface by providing accessible design patterns and interactive elements that cater to users with diverse needs and preferences.

Characteristics of UI Components

UI components exhibit several key characteristics that distinguish them from ad-hoc design elements:

1. **Reusability**

   UI components are designed to be reusable across different projects and contexts. Once created, a UI component can be replicated and used throughout the interface, saving time and effort for designers and ensuring consistency and coherence in the design.

2. **Consistency**

   UI components promote consistency in design by providing standardized solutions to common design problems. By using consistent components throughout an interface, designers can create a cohesive and unified user experience that is easy to navigate and understand.

3. **Flexibility**

   While UI components provide a standardized solution to a design problem, they also allow for flexibility and customization. Designers can customize components to fit the specific context and requirements of their project, ensuring that the design meets the needs of the target audience.

In conclusion, UI components are essential elements of UI design, providing designers with reusable solutions to common design problems and interaction challenges. By leveraging UI components effectively, designers can create interfaces that are not only visually appealing but also functional, intuitive, and consistent. However, it's essential for designers to use components thoughtfully and appropriately, considering the specific needs and preferences of their target audience and customizing components to fit the unique context and requirements of their project. With careful planning and execution, designers can create interfaces that deliver a seamless and enjoyable user experience.

Common UI Components

User Interface (UI) components are essential elements of digital design, providing designers with modular building blocks to create visually appealing and functional interfaces. Here, we will explore some of the most common UI components used across various digital platforms, discussing their characteristics, applications, and best practices for implementation.

Buttons

Buttons are interactive elements that allow users to perform actions or navigate to different parts of the interface. They are often used to initiate primary or secondary actions, such as submitting a form, opening a link, or triggering a modal dialog. Buttons come in various styles, including:

1. **Primary Buttons:** Primary buttons are typically used for the most important actions in the interface, such as submitting a form or completing a purchase. They are often styled with bold colors or prominent icons to draw attention to them.
2. **Secondary Buttons:** Secondary buttons are used for less critical actions or as alternative options to the primary action. They are usually styled with less prominent colors or simpler designs to differentiate them from primary buttons.
3. **Icon Buttons:** Icon buttons contain only an icon or a small graphic and are commonly used for actions that have a clear visual representation, such as a trash can icon for deleting an item or a heart icon for adding to favorites.

Buttons should be designed with clear visual cues and affordances to indicate their interactive nature. They should also be accessible and responsive to different input methods, such as mouse clicks, touch gestures, and keyboard navigation.

Cards

Cards are versatile containers used to present content in a visually appealing and digestible format. They typically consist of a rectangular or square-shaped container with content inside, such as text, images, or other multimedia elements. Cards are commonly used for:

1. **Content Display:** Cards are often used to showcase individual pieces of content, such as articles, products, or user profiles. Each card contains a summary or preview of the content, along with a thumbnail image and relevant metadata.

2. **Grouping Content:** Cards can also be used to group related content together, such as a collection of articles or products. By organizing content into cards, designers can create a visually pleasing layout that makes it easy for users to scan and navigate through the interface.

3. **Interactive Elements:** Cards can contain interactive elements, such as buttons or links, allowing users to take actions directly from the card. For example, a product card may include a "Buy Now" button that users can click to purchase the item.Cards should be designed with a consistent layout and visual style to maintain cohesion and clarity across the interface. They should also be responsive to different screen sizes and orientations, ensuring that they display effectively on a variety of devices and viewport sizes.

In conclusion, buttons and cards are just two examples of the many UI components that designers use to create engaging and intuitive interfaces. By understanding the characteristics and applications of these components, designers can effectively leverage them to create interfaces that are both visually appealing and functional.

UI patterns and components are indispensable tools for designers and developers, providing them with reusable solutions to common design problems and interface challenges. By incorporating UI patterns and components into their designs, designers can streamline the design process, improve usability, and create interfaces that are both visually appealing and functional. However, it's essential for designers to use patterns and components thoughtfully and appropriately, considering the specific needs and preferences of their target audience and customizing patterns and components to fit the unique context and requirements of the project. With careful planning, testing, and iteration, designers can create interfaces that are intuitive, consistent, and engaging, providing users with an optimal user experience.

CHAPTER SIX

Visual Design Techniques

❝

Simplicity is about subtracting the obvious and adding the meaningful

Visual design plays a crucial role in creating engaging and effective user interfaces. It encompasses a wide range of principles, techniques, and tools aimed at enhancing the aesthetic appeal, usability, and overall user experience of digital products. In this chapter, we will explore various visual design techniques used by designers to create visually compelling interfaces.

Understanding Visual Hierarchy

Visual hierarchy is a fundamental principle in design that guides the viewer's attention and prioritizes information within a layout. It involves arranging elements in a way that establishes their relative importance and guides the viewer's eye through the design in a deliberate sequence. One of the primary techniques used to establish visual hierarchy is through the strategic use of visual attributes such as size, color, contrast, typography, and spacing. Larger, bolder, or more prominently positioned elements are perceived as more important, while smaller or less prominent elements are perceived as secondary or tertiary. By leveraging these visual cues, designers can create clear and intuitive layouts that draw the viewer's attention to key elements and guide them through the content in a logical and engaging manner.

Establishing Importance

Establishing importance is one of the primary functions of visual hierarchy. By strategically emphasizing certain elements over others, designers can draw the viewer's attention to key pieces of information or actions within the interface. For example, using larger or bolder typography for headings and titles can help establish their importance and make them stand out from the surrounding text. Similarly, using vibrant colors or high-contrast combinations for important elements can draw attention to them and make them more visually prominent. By establishing importance, designers can ensure that users quickly understand the most critical aspects of the interface and can easily navigate to the desired content or actions.

Organizing Information

Visual hierarchy also plays a crucial role in organizing information within a layout. By structuring elements in a hierarchical order, designers can create a clear and intuitive flow of information that guides users through the interface in a logical sequence. For example, using larger headings and subheadings to break up content into distinct sections can help users understand the overall structure of the page and locate specific information more efficiently.

Similarly, using consistent spacing and alignment techniques can help create a sense of order and cohesion within the layout, making it easier for users to scan and digest the content. By organizing information effectively, designers can enhance the usability and readability of the interface, leading to a more positive user experience.

Directing Focus

Another crucial aspect of visual hierarchy is its ability to direct the viewer's focus and guide them through the interface. By strategically emphasizing certain elements and de-emphasizing others, designers can control the viewer's attention and ensure that they engage with the most important parts of the design first. For example, using contrasting colors or bold typography for call-to-action buttons can draw attention to them and encourage users to take specific actions. Similarly, using visual cues such as arrows or icons can direct the viewer's gaze towards relevant content or interactive elements. By directing focus, designers can create interfaces that are more intuitive and engaging, leading to improved user satisfaction and conversion rates.

Creating Harmony

In addition to establishing importance, organizing information, and directing focus, visual hierarchy also plays a crucial role in creating harmony within the design. By balancing the visual weight of different elements and maintaining a sense of order and cohesion, designers can create layouts that are visually pleasing and easy to understand. For example, using a consistent color scheme or typeface throughout the interface can help create a sense of unity and coherence, tying the design together and making it feel more polished and professional. Similarly, using proportional spacing and alignment techniques can help create a sense of balance and rhythm within the layout, reducing visual clutter and improving readability. By creating harmony, designers can ensure that the interface feels cohesive and well-designed, enhancing the overall user experience.

In conclusion, visual hierarchy is a critical aspect of design that guides the viewer's attention, organizes information, directs focus, and creates harmony within the interface. By strategically leveraging visual attributes such as size, color, contrast, typography, and spacing, designers can create layouts that are intuitive, engaging, and visually appealing. By understanding the principles of visual hierarchy and applying them effectively in their designs, designers can create interfaces that not only look great but also enhance the overall user experience. With careful planning, experimentation, and iteration, designers can leverage visual hierarchy to create interfaces that captivate and delight users, leading to increased engagement, satisfaction, and success.

Color Theory and Psychology

Color theory is a fundamental concept in design that explores the principles behind how colors interact with each other and how they can be used to create visually appealing and harmonious compositions. Understanding color theory is essential for designers as it allows them to make informed decisions about color palettes, create visual hierarchy, and evoke specific emotions or responses in their audience. Additionally, color psychology examines how different colors can influence human perception, emotions, and behavior, providing valuable insights into how color choices can impact the user experience.

The Basics of Color Theory

At its core, color theory revolves around the color wheel, which is a visual representation of the relationships between different colors. The color wheel is divided into primary colors (red, blue, and yellow), secondary colors (green, orange, and purple), and tertiary colors (created by mixing primary and secondary colors). Designers use color theory principles such as complementary colors (opposite each other on the color wheel), analogous colors (adjacent to each other), and triadic colors (equally spaced around the wheel) to create harmonious color schemes that balance contrast and cohesion.

The Role of Color Contrast

Color contrast is another crucial aspect of color theory, referring to the difference in brightness, hue, or saturation between different colors. High-contrast combinations create visual interest and make elements stand out from their surroundings, while low-contrast combinations create a more subtle and cohesive look. Designers use contrast strategically to draw attention to key elements, create emphasis, and improve readability. For example, using a dark text color on a light background or vice versa ensures sufficient contrast for easy readability, while using complementary colors for accents or call-to-action buttons creates visual impact and draws attention.

Color Harmonies and Schemes

Color harmonies, also known as color schemes or color combinations, are predetermined combinations of colors that are aesthetically pleasing when used together. Some common color harmonies include:

1. **Complementary:** Colors that are opposite each other on the color wheel, such as red and green or blue and orange. Complementary colors create strong contrast and can make each other appear more vibrant when used together.

2. **Analogous:** Colors that are adjacent to each other on the color wheel, such as blue, green, and teal. Analogous colors create a sense of harmony and cohesion and are often used to create subtle and unified color schemes.

3. **Triadic:** Colors that are equally spaced around the color wheel, such as red, yellow, and blue. Triadic color schemes are vibrant and dynamic, offering a good balance of contrast and harmony.

The Psychology of Color

Color psychology explores how different colors can evoke specific emotions, associations, and responses in viewers. While color perception can vary depending on cultural, personal, and contextual factors, certain colors are commonly associated with specific meanings and emotions. For example:

1. **Red:** Often associated with energy, passion, and excitement, red can create a sense of urgency or importance. It is commonly used for calls to action or to evoke feelings of intensity and vitality.
2. **Blue:** Symbolizing calmness, stability, and trustworthiness, blue is often used in corporate branding and healthcare contexts to convey a sense of reliability and professionalism.
3. **Yellow:** Representing optimism, happiness, and warmth, yellow is often used to evoke feelings of cheerfulness and positivity. It can be effective for grabbing attention or conveying a sense of playfulness.

Cultural and Contextual Considerations

While certain colors may have universal associations, it's essential to consider cultural and contextual factors when choosing colors for design projects. Colors can have different meanings and symbolism in different cultures, and what may be perceived positively in one culture may have negative connotations in another. Additionally, the context in which colors and harmony.

Which is used can influence their interpretation and impact. For example, a red color scheme may convey excitement and energy in a sports app but may be perceived as alarming or aggressive in a healthcare app. Designers should be mindful of cultural sensitivities and the specific context of their projects when selecting colors to ensure that they resonate with their target audience and effectively communicate the intended message.

Applying Color Theory in Design

In practice, designers apply color theory principles to create visually appealing and effective designs that resonate with their audience. By understanding the basics of color theory, designers can:

1. **Create Harmonious Color Schemes:** By using complementary, analogous, or triadic color schemes, designers can create visually pleasing compositions that balance contrast and cohesion.
2. **Establish Visual Hierarchy:** Designers use color to establish visual hierarchy and guide the viewer's attention through the interface. By using contrasting colors for important elements and muted colors for background elements, designers can create clear and intuitive layouts that prioritize key information.
3. **Evoke Emotions and Responses:** Designers leverage color psychology to evoke specific emotions or associations in their audience. By choosing colors that align with the desired mood or message of the design, designers can create more impactful and memorable experiences for users.

In conclusion, color theory and psychology are essential aspects of design that influence how colors are used to create visually compelling and emotionally resonant experiences. By understanding the principles of color theory, designers can create harmonious color schemes, establish visual hierarchy, and evoke specific emotions or responses in their audience. However, it's crucial for designers to consider cultural and contextual factors when choosing colors for their projects to ensure that they resonate with their target audience and effectively communicate the intended message. With careful planning and consideration, designers can leverage color theory and psychology to create designs that are not only visually appealing but also meaningful and impactful.

Typography and Typeface Selection

Typography plays a crucial role in design, influencing readability, user experience, and visual appeal. Typeface selection, font pairing, and typographic hierarchy are all essential considerations for designers when crafting interfaces, websites, and printed materials. This chapter delves into the intricacies of typography and provides insights into effective typeface selection techniques.

Understanding Typography

Typography encompasses the art and technique of arranging typefaces to make written language readable and visually appealing. It involves selecting appropriate fonts, sizes, weights, and styles to communicate information effectively. Good typography enhances the readability of text, guides users through content, and establishes the overall tone and personality of a design. Designers must consider factors such as line spacing, line length, and font size to optimize readability and legibility across different devices and screen sizes.

The Role of Typeface Selection

Typeface selection is a critical aspect of typography, influencing the mood, tone, and readability of a design. Each typeface has its own personality and characteristics, which can evoke different emotions and associations in viewers. Serif typefaces, characterized by small decorative flourishes at the ends of strokes, convey a sense of tradition, elegance, and authority, making them suitable for formal or classic designs. Sans-serif typefaces, on the other hand, are more modern, clean, and straightforward, making them ideal for contemporary or minimalist designs. Designers must carefully consider the context, audience, and message of a design when selecting typefaces to ensure that they align with the intended tone and purpose.

Font Pairing Techniques

Font pairing involves combining two or more typefaces to create visual contrast and harmony in a design. Effective font pairing techniques can enhance readability, establish hierarchy, and add visual interest to a layout. Designers often pair contrasting typefaces to create a dynamic and balanced composition. For example, pairing a bold, display typeface with a subtle, sans-serif body font can create a striking contrast that draws attention to headlines and titles while maintaining readability in body text. Designers must consider factors such as x-height, stroke weight, and letter spacing when pairing typefaces to ensure that they complement each other and create a cohesive visual experience.

Establishing Typographic Hierarchy

Typographic hierarchy refers to the organization and prioritization of text elements within a design to guide users' attention and emphasize important information. Designers use techniques such as font size, weight, style, and color to establish typographic hierarchy and create a clear visual structure. Headings, subheadings, body text, and captions are all examples of typographic elements that can be differentiated through size, weight, or style to convey their relative importance. Designers must consider the content hierarchy, user goals, and reading patterns when establishing typographic hierarchy to ensure that users can quickly scan and understand the information presented.

Responsive Typography

Responsive typography is the practice of adjusting typography to accommodate different screen sizes, resolutions, and orientations. With the proliferation of mobile devices and varying viewport sizes, responsive typography has become increasingly important in ensuring that text remains legible and readable across different devices and contexts. Designers use techniques such as fluid typography, viewport units, and media queries to adapt typography to different screen sizes and resolutions dynamically. By prioritizing readability and legibility, designers can create responsive typography that enhances the user experience and ensures accessibility for all users.

Accessibility Considerations

Accessibility is an essential consideration in typography, ensuring that text is legible and readable for users with visual impairments or disabilities. Designers must consider factors such as font size, contrast ratio, and letter spacing to improve readability and ensure that text is accessible to all users. Guidelines such as the Web

Content Accessibility Guidelines (WCAG) provide recommendations for typography accessibility, including minimum font sizes, contrast ratios, and line spacing requirements. By adhering to accessibility guidelines, designers can create inclusive designs that are accessible to a diverse range of users.

In conclusion, typography plays a crucial role in design, influencing readability, user experience, and visual appeal. Typeface selection, font pairing, typographic hierarchy, and responsive typography are all essential considerations for designers when crafting interfaces, websites, and printed materials. By understanding the principles of typography and applying effective typeface selection techniques, designers can create visually compelling designs that communicate information effectively and engage users. With careful consideration of typography, designers can enhance the overall user experience and create designs that are both aesthetically pleasing and functional.

Layout and Composition Techniques

Layout and composition are fundamental aspects of design, influencing the organization, structure, and visual hierarchy of a composition. Effective layout and composition techniques help designers create visually appealing and functional designs that guide users through content and convey information effectively. This chapter explores various layout and composition techniques used by designers to create compelling designs.

Understanding Layout

Layout refers to the arrangement and organization of visual elements within a design. It involves determining the placement, size, and spacing of elements to create a balanced and harmonious composition. Layouts can vary in complexity, ranging from simple grids to more elaborate arrangements. Grid-based layouts are a common approach to organizing content, providing a structured framework that facilitates alignment, consistency, and visual hierarchy. Designers must consider factors such as content hierarchy, user goals, and reading patterns when creating layouts to ensure that information is presented in a logical and intuitive manner.

Principles of Balance

Balance is a fundamental principle of design that involves distributing visual weight evenly across a composition. There are three main types of balance: symmetrical, asymmetrical, and radial. Symmetrical balance involves arranging elements evenly on either side of a central axis, creating a sense of stability and order. Asymmetrical balance involves distributing visual weight unequally to create a more dynamic and engaging composition. Radial balance involves arranging elements around a central point, creating a circular or spiral pattern. Designers use balance to create a sense of harmony and unity within a composition, ensuring that elements work together cohesively.

Alignment Techniques

Alignment refers to the positioning of elements relative to each other within a composition. Proper alignment helps create order and cohesion, making a design easier to navigate and understand. There are four main types of alignment: left, right, center, and justified. Left alignment is the most common and involves aligning elements along the left edge of the composition. Right alignment is less common and involves aligning elements along the right edge. Center alignment involves aligning elements along a central axis, creating a sense of balance and symmetry. Justified alignment involves aligning elements along both the left and right edges, creating a straight, clean edge on both sides. Designers use alignment to create a sense of unity and organization within a composition, ensuring that elements are visually connected and related to each other.

Creating Visual Flow

Visual flow refers to the path that a viewer's eye follows as they move through a composition. Designers use various techniques to create visual flow, such as leading lines, directional cues, and focal points. Leading lines are lines that lead the viewer's eye from one part of the composition to another, creating a sense of movement and direction. Directional cues, such as arrows or gestures, indicate where the viewer should look or how they should navigate through the composition. Focal points are areas of interest within a composition that draw the viewer's attention and anchor the visual flow. By creating visual flow, designers can guide users through content and ensure that information is presented in a clear and intuitive manner.

White Space and Negative Space

White space, also known as negative space, refers to the empty space between elements within a composition. It plays a crucial role in design, providing visual breathing room and enhancing readability and comprehension. White space helps create a sense of balance, contrast, and emphasis within a composition, making it easier for users to focus on key elements and understand the overall structure of the design. Designers use white space strategically to improve clarity, hierarchy, and aesthetics, ensuring that a composition feels open, inviting, and well-balanced.

Repetition and Consistency

Repetition and consistency are essential principles of design that help create unity, cohesion, and rhythm within a composition. Repetition involves using consistent visual elements, such as colors, shapes, or patterns, throughout a composition to create a sense of unity and reinforce key themes or messages. Consistency involves maintaining a uniform style, layout, and structure across different parts of a composition or design system. By using repetition and consistency, designers can create designs that are cohesive, harmonious, and easy to navigate, ensuring a positive user experience. In conclusion, layout and composition are critical aspects of design that influence the organization, structure, and visual hierarchy of a composition. By understanding principles such as balance, alignment, visual flow, white space, repetition, and consistency, designers can create visually appealing and functional designs that guide users through content and convey information effectively. With careful consideration of layout and composition techniques, designers can create compelling designs that engage users, communicate messages, and achieve desired goals. aesthetics, ensuring that a composition feels open, inviting, and well-balanced.

Visual Consistency and Branding

Repetition and Consistency

Visual consistency and branding are essential elements of design that contribute to a cohesive and memorable user experience. Consistency in visual elements such as colors, typography, imagery, and layout helps create a unified look and feel across different parts of a design or brand identity. Branding extends beyond visual elements to encompass the overall perception and personality of a brand, including its values, messaging, and customer interactions. This chapter explores the importance of visual consistency and branding in design and provides insights into how designers can create cohesive brand experiences.

Importance of Visual Consistency

Visual consistency plays a crucial role in design by providing users with a familiar and predictable experience. Consistent visual elements help users navigate interfaces more easily, find information quickly, and understand the overall structure of a design. When elements such as colors, typography, and layout remain consistent across different screens or pages, users are less likely to feel confused or disoriented. Visual consistency also helps reinforce brand identity and build trust with users, as it signals professionalism, attention to detail, and reliability. By maintaining visual consistency, designers can create designs that are intuitive, user-friendly, and memorable.

Establishing Brand Identity

Brand identity encompasses the visual and verbal elements that define a brand and differentiate it from competitors. These elements include logos, colors, typography, imagery, and messaging, among others. A strong brand identity communicates the values, personality, and essence of a brand, helping it connect with customers on an emotional level. Designers play a crucial role in establishing and maintaining brand identity by creating visual assets that reflect the brand's values and resonate with its target audience. Consistency is key to building a strong brand identity, as it ensures that all brand touchpoints, from websites and mobile apps to marketing materials and packaging, align with the brand's overarching vision and messaging.

Guidelines for Visual Consistency

Designers can maintain visual consistency by following a set of guidelines or brand standards that outline the rules and principles for using visual elements. These guidelines typically include specifications for colors, typography, logo usage, imagery, and layout, as well as rules for maintaining consistency across different mediums and channAels. By adhering to these guidelines, designers can ensure that all visual elements align with the brand's identity and contribute to a cohesive brand experience. Consistent use of colors, typography, and imagery helps reinforce brand recognition and make the brand more memorable to users.

Building Brand Trust

Consistent branding builds trust with users by creating a sense of familiarity and reliability. When users encounter consistent visual elements across different touchpoints, they perceive the brand as more professional, established, and trustworthy. Consistent branding also helps reinforce brand values and messaging, which can resonate with users on a deeper level. By consistently delivering on its promises and maintaining a coherent brand identity, a brand can foster long-term relationships with its audience and establish itself as a leader in its industry.

Implementing Branding Across Channels

Branding consistency is particularly important in today's multi-channel digital landscape, where users interact with brands across a variety of platforms and devices. Whether it's a website, mobile app, social media platform, or physical storefront, maintaining consistent branding across channels helps reinforce the brand's identity and create a seamless user experience. Designers must adapt brand elements to different mediums and contexts while ensuring that they remain true to the brand's overarching vision and values. Consistent use of colors, typography, imagery, and messaging helps users recognize and connect with the brand, regardless of the channel or device they are using.

Evolving Brand Identity

While consistency is essential for building a strong brand identity, brands must also be adaptable and responsive to changing market trends and consumer preferences. As brands evolve and grow, they may need to update their visual identity to stay relevant and resonate with their target audience. Designers play a crucial role in evolving brand identity by refreshing visual elements, experimenting with new design trends, and maintaining consistency while embracing innovation. By striking the right balance between consistency and evolution, brands can remain relevant and competitive in an ever-changing marketplace.

In conclusion, visual consistency and branding are essential components of design that contribute to a cohesive and memorable user experience. By maintaining consistency in visual elements such as colors, typography, imagery, and layout, designers can create designs that are intuitive, user-friendly, and reflective of the brand's identity. Consistent branding builds trust with users and reinforces brand values and messaging, fostering long-term relationships and brand loyalty. By following guidelines for visual consistency and adapting brand elements to different channels and contexts, designers can create compelling brand experiences that resonate with users and drive business success.

In conclusion, visual design techniques are essential for creating engaging, intuitive, and visually appealing user experience. By maintaining consistency in visual elements such as colors, typography, imagery, and layout, designers can create designs that are intuitive, user-friendly, and reflective of the brand's identity. Consistent branding builds trust with users and reinforces brand values and messaging, fostering long-term relationships and brand loyalty. By following guidelines for visual consistency and adapting brand elements to different channels and contexts, designers can create compelling brand experiences that resonate with users and drive business success.

CHAPTER SEVEN

UI Animation For Engagement

> "
>
> Design creates culture. Culture shapes values. Values determine the future.

UI animation is a powerful tool for enhancing user engagement and creating memorable digital experiences. When used strategically, animations can draw users' attention, guide them through interfaces, and provide feedback, resulting in increased interactivity and satisfaction. This chapter explores the role of UI animation in engagement and provides insights into how designers can leverage animation techniques effectively.

Visual Consistency and Branding

UI animation is a fundamental component of modern digital design, playing a pivotal role in enhancing user experience and engagement. It goes beyond mere decoration, serving as a powerful tool for communication, feedback, and guiding user interactions. Animation provides visual cues that inform users about changes in interface states, transitions between screens, and the outcome of their actions. By adding motion to static elements, UI animation breathes life into interfaces, making them more dynamic and intuitive for users to navigate.

One of the key aspects of UI animation is its ability to improve usability by providing clear feedback and context to users. For instance, animated transitions between screens help users understand the spatial relationship between different interface elements, reducing cognitive load and making interactions more fluid. Similarly, microinteractions, such as button presses or form submissions, can be enhanced with subtle animations that provide immediate feedback, reinforcing the user's actions and creating a more responsive experience.

Moreover, UI animation contributes to the overall aesthetics of a design, adding personality and charm to interfaces. Thoughtfully designed animations can evoke emotions, convey brand identity, and create memorable experiences for users. Whether it's a playful loading animation or a smooth transition effect, animation has the power to delight users and leave a lasting impression. By incorporating animation into their designs, designers can differentiate their products in a crowded marketplace and forge stronger emotional connections with users.

In addition to improving usability and aesthetics, UI animation also has practical benefits for designers and developers. Animation can help bridge the gap between design and development by providing a tangible representation of interaction concepts. Prototyping animations allows designers to communicate their vision more effectively to stakeholders and developers, facilitating collaboration and iteration throughout the design process. Furthermore, animation libraries and frameworks enable developers to implement complex interactions with ease, reducing development time and effort.

Overall, UI animation is an indispensable tool for creating engaging and user-friendly digital experiences. From enhancing usability and aesthetics to facilitating collaboration between designers and developers, animation has a wide range of applications in modern digital design. As technology continues to evolve, the importance of UI animation will only grow, offering new opportunities for designers to innovate and delight users with immersive and interactive interfaces.

Types of UI Animation

UI animation encompasses a variety of animation techniques that serve different purposes in digital design. Each type of animation has its own characteristics and applications, ranging from providing feedback to guiding user interactions. Understanding the different types of UI animation is essential for designers to effectively communicate ideas, enhance usability, and create engaging user experiences.

1. **Transitions:** Transitions are animations that occur when moving between different states or screens within an interface. They provide continuity and context to user interactions, making navigation more intuitive and seamless. Common transition effects include fades, slides, and flips.

2. **Microinteractions:** Microinteractions are small, subtle animations that provide feedback or communicate status to users. They occur in response to specific user actions, such as button presses or form submissions, and help reinforce the user's actions. Examples of microinteractions include button animations, loading spinners, and hover effects, which enhance usability and engagement.

3. **Scroll-based animations:** Scroll-based animations change elements of the interface as users scroll through content, creating a dynamic and interactive experience. These animations can include parallax effects, fade-ins, or transformations that respond to the user's scrolling behavior. Scroll-based animations help engage users and draw attention to important content, making browsing more engaging and enjoyable.

4. **Hover animations:** Hover animations respond to user hover actions, providing visual feedback and enhancing interactivity. When users hover over interactive elements, such as buttons or links, they trigger animations that indicate the element's state or behavior. Hover animations can include

color changes, enlargements, or subtle movements, which help users understand the interactive nature of the element.

5. **Loading animations:** Loading animations entertain users during wait times and indicate that the system is processing their request. They prevent users from feeling bored or frustrated while waiting for content to load and provide reassurance that their action has been acknowledged.

6. **Progress animations:** Progress animations visually communicate the progress of a task or process to users. They provide feedback on the status of an operation, such as file uploads, downloads, or form submissions, and help users understand the time remaining or completion status. Progress animations can include progress bars, spinners, or percentage indicators, which keep users informed and engaged throughout the process.

In conclusion, understanding the different types of UI animation allows designers to leverage animation effectively to enhance usability, engagement, and overall user experience. Whether it's providing feedback, guiding interactions, or entertaining users during wait times, animation plays a crucial role in modern digital design. By incorporating animation into their designs thoughtfully and purposefully, designers can create interfaces that are not only functional but also delightful and memorable for users.

Principles of Effective UI Animation

UI animation is a critical aspect of modern digital design, contributing significantly to user experience and engagement.

Effective UI animation relies on several key principles that guide its implementation, ensuring that animations are purposeful, performant, and user-friendly. These principles play a crucial role in creating animations that enhance usability, communicate effectively, and delight users.

1. **Purposeful Animation:** Every animation within a user interface should serve a clear purpose and add value to the user experience. Purposeful animations provide feedback, guide navigation, or enhance visual appeal, improving usability and engagement. Designers should avoid using animations solely for decorative purposes and instead focus on animations that serve a functional or communicative purpose.

2. **Performance Optimization:** Performance optimization is essential for ensuring smooth and responsive animations across different devices and platforms. Optimizing animation involves minimizing computational overhead, reducing animation complexity, and leveraging hardware acceleration where available. By prioritizing performance, designers can create animations that enhance user experience without compromising performance.

3. **Consistency and Coherence:** Consistency is key to creating a cohesive and intuitive user experience. Animations should be consistent with the overall design language and branding of the interface, maintaining coherence and familiarity for users. Designers should use consistent timing, easing curves,

and visual styles across different animations to create a unified and harmonious experience.

4. **Relevance to Context:** Animation should be contextually relevant and support the user's goals and tasks within the interface. Contextually relevant animations enhance usability and provide valuable feedback to users, guiding them through interactions and tasks. Designers should consider the user's context and intentions.

5. **Accessibility and Inclusivity:** Animation should be inclusive and accessible to all users, including those with disabilities. Accessible animations provide alternative means of interaction for users who may have difficulty with animated content and do not rely solely on visual cues. Designers should consider factors such as motion sensitivity, cognitive impairments, and screen reader compatibility when designing animations to ensure accessibility for all users.

6. **Usability Testing and Iteration:** Usability testing is essential for evaluating the effectiveness of animations and gathering feedback from users. By testing animations with users, designers can identify areas for improvement and iterate on designs based on user responses. Usability testing helps ensure that animations enhance rather than hinder user experience and allows designers to refine animations iteratively for optimal usability and engagement.

In conclusion, adhering to these principles of effective UI animation is crucial for creating animations that enhance usability, engagement, and overall user experience. By ensuring that animations are purposeful, performant, consistent, relevant, accessible, and tested iteratively, designers can leverage animation as a powerful tool for creating compelling and delightful digital experiences that delight users and drive business success.

Best Practices for UI Animation

UI animation has become an integral part of modern digital design, offering designers a powerful tool to enhance user experience and engagement. However, to leverage animation effectively, designers must follow best practices that ensure animations are purposeful, intuitive, and user-friendly. These best practices guide the creation and implementation of UI animation, helping designers create animations that add value to the user experience without overwhelming or distracting users.

1. **Purposeful Animation:**

   Every animation within a user interface should serve a clear purpose and provide value to the user. Purposeful animations enhance usability, communicate feedback, or guide user interactions, improving overall user experience. Designers should avoid using animations solely for decorative purposes and instead focus on animations that serve a functional or communicative purpose.

2. **Performance Optimization:**

   Performance optimization is essential for ensuring smooth and responsive animations across different devices and platforms. Optimizing animation involves minimizing computational overhead, reducing animation complexity, and leveraging hardware acceleration where available. By prioritizing performance, designers can create animations that enhance user experience without compromising performance.

3. **Consistency and Coherence:**

Consistency is key to creating a cohesive and intuitive user experience. Animations should be consistent with the overall design language and branding of the interface, maintaining coherence and familiarity for users. Designers should use consistent timing, easing curves, and visual styles across different animations to create a unified and harmonious experience.

4. **Relevance to Context:**

Animation should be contextually relevant and support the user's goals and tasks within the interface. Contextually relevant animations enhance usability and provide valuable feedback to users, guiding them through interactions and tasks. Designers should consider the user's context and intentions when designing animations to ensure they align with user expectations and behaviors.

5. **Accessibility and Inclusivity:**

Animation should be inclusive and accessible to all users, including those with disabilities. Accessible animations provide alternative means of interaction for users who may have difficulty with animated content and do not rely solely on visual cues. Designers should consider factors such as motion sensitivity, cognitive impairments, and screen reader compatibility when designing animations to ensure accessibility for all users.

6. **Usability Testing and Iteration:**

Usability testing is essential for evaluating the effectiveness of animations and gathering feedback from users. By testing animations with users, designers can identify areas for improvement and iterate on designs based on user responses. Usability testing helps ensure that animations enhance rather than hinder user experience and allows designers.

7. **Start with a Storyboard:**

Before implementing animations in a user interface, designers should create a storyboard that outlines the purpose, timing, and sequence of animations. Storyboarding helps designers plan animations effectively and ensures that animations align with user goals and tasks. By starting with a storyboard, designers can create animations that are purposeful and intuitive, enhancing overall user experience.

8. **Keep it Subtle:**

When designing animations, it's essential to keep them subtle and unobtrusive. Avoid overly flashy or distracting animations that may overwhelm users or detract from the user experience. Instead, focus on animations that provide clear feedback and enhance usability without drawing too much attention to themselves. Subtle animations contribute to a polished and intuitive user experience, making interactions more enjoyable for users.

9. **Use Easing Curves:**

Easing curves control the acceleration and deceleration of animations, influencing how they feel and behave. Designers should use easing curves to create animations that feel natural and intuitive, avoiding abrupt or jarring movements. By adjusting easing curves, designers can fine-tune animations to match the desired user experience, creating animations that are smooth and responsive.

10. **Test Across Devices and Platforms:**

Animations may behave differently across different devices and platforms, leading to inconsistencies in user experience. Designers should test animations across various devices and platforms to ensure consistent behavior and performance.

11. **Iterate Based on Feedback:**

Gathering feedback from users is essential for evaluating the effectiveness of animations and identifying areas for improvement. Designers should iterate on animations based on user feedback, making adjustments to timing, duration, and visual style as needed. By iterating based on feedback, designers can refine animations iteratively, ensuring that they enhance rather than hinder user experience.

12. Document Animation Guidelines:

Documenting animation guidelines helps ensure consistency and coherence across different animations within a user interface. Animation guidelines should outline rules and principles for using animation, including specifications for timing, easing curves, and visual styles. By documenting animation guidelines, designers can maintain consistency and coherence in animations, creating a unified and harmonious user experience.

13. Consider Performance Impact:

Animation can impact performance, especially on low-powered devices or slow internet connections. Designers should consider the performance impact of animations and prioritize performance optimization to ensure smooth and responsive user experience. By optimizing animations for performance, designers can create animations that enhance user experience without compromising performance.

14. Educate Stakeholders:

Educating stakeholders about the benefits and best practices of UI animation is essential for gaining buy-in and support for animation projects. In conclusion, following best practices for UI animation is essential for creating animations that enhance usability, engagement, and overall user experience. By ensuring that animations are purposeful, performant, consistent, relevant, accessible, and tested iteratively, designers can leverage animation as a powerful tool for creating compelling and delightful digital experiences. By incorporating best practices into their animation projects, designers can create animations that delight users, drive engagement, and contribute to the success of digital products and services.

Examples of UI Animation in Action

UI animation plays a vital role in enhancing user experience and engagement across a wide range of digital products and services. By incorporating animations thoughtfully and purposefully, designers can create interfaces that are not only functional but also delightful and memorable for users. Let's explore some examples of UI animation in action, highlighting how animations are used to improve usability, communicate feedback, and create immersive experiences for users.

1. **Loading Animations:**

    Loading animations provide visual feedback to users while they wait for content to load, reducing perceived wait times and preventing user frustration. For example, the loading animation used by Google's Chrome browser features a spinning circle that indicates the progress of page loading.

2. Microinteractions:

Microinteractions are small, subtle animations that occur in response to user actions, providing feedback and guidance throughout the user journey. For instance, the heart animation used by Instagram when users like a post is a microinteraction that reinforces user actions and adds delight to the user experience. This animation appears instantly when users tap the heart icon, providing immediate feedback and enhancing engagement with the platform.

3. Scroll-Based Animations:

Scroll-based animations respond to the user's scrolling behavior, creating dynamic and interactive experiences as users navigate through content. The "parallax scrolling" effect used by Apple's website is a prime example of scroll-based animation. As users scroll down the page, background images move at different speeds, creating a sense of depth and immersion. This captivating animation draws users' attention and encourages them to explore the website further.

4. Transition Effects:

Transition effects are used to smoothly transition between different states or screens within an interface, improving continuity and flow. The "material design" transition effect used by Google's Material Design system is a widely recognized example of effective transition animation. When users navigate between screens or elements, they observe subtle animations such as fades, slides, and morphs, which create a seamless transition experience. These animations help users understand the spatial relationships between different interface elements and maintain context as they navigate through the interface.

5. Feedback Animations:

Feedback animations provide visual cues to users in response to their actions, helping them understand the outcome of their interactions. The "shake" animation used by password input fields in many mobile applications is a classic example of feedback animation. When users enter an incorrect password, the input field shakes from side to side, indicating that the input was invalid. This animation communicates feedback to users instantly, helping them correct errors and proceed with their tasks.

6. Interactive Widgets:

Interactive widgets leverage animation to enhance user interactions and make interfaces more engaging and intuitive. The "swipe to delete" gesture used by mobile email applications is a prime example of an interactive widget with animation. When users swipe left on an email, it triggers an animation that reveals a delete button, allowing users to delete the email with a single gesture. This animation simplifies the deletion process and adds a layer of interactivity to the interface, improving user experience.

7. Navigation Animations:

Navigation animations guide users through interfaces and provide visual cues that aid in orientation and exploration. The "bottom navigation bar" used by many mobile applications features navigation icons that animate when selected, indicating the current active state. As users switch between navigation tabs, the selected tab expands or changes color, providing clear visual feedback and helping users understand their location within the app.

In conclusion, these examples demonstrate the diverse applications of UI animation in modern digital design, showcasing how animation can enhance usability, engagement, and overall user experience. By incorporating animations thoughtfully and purposefully, designers can create interfaces that are not only functional but also delightful and memorable for users. As technology continues to evolve, the role of UI animation in digital design will only grow, offering new opportunities for designers to innovate and create immersive experiences that captivate users and drive business success.

Implementing UI Animation in Design

Implementing UI animation in design requires careful consideration of various factors, including purpose, performance, and user experience. By following a systematic approach, designers can effectively incorporate animations into their designs to enhance usability, engagement, and overall user experience.

1. Define Animation Goals:

The first step in implementing UI animation is to define clear goals for the animations. What purpose do the animations serve? Are they intended to provide feedback, guide navigation, or enhance visual appeal? By identifying the goals of the animations, designers can ensure that animations align with user needs and contribute to the overall design objectives perspective on their nature.

2. Storyboard Animations:

Once the goals of the animations are defined, designers should create storyboards that outline the sequence, timing, and behavior of the animations. Storyboarding helps designers visualize how animations will unfold within the interface and ensures that animations are purposeful and intuitive. By storyboarding animations, designers can plan animations effectively and communicate their vision.

3. Choose the Right Tools:

Designers have a variety of tools at their disposal for creating animations, ranging from prototyping tools to animation libraries and frameworks. Depending on the complexity of the animations and the designer's familiarity with different tools, designers should choose the right tools that best suit their needs. Whether it's using prototyping tools to create interactive prototypes or leveraging animation libraries to implement complex interactions, choosing the right tools is essential for successful animation implementation.

4. Iterate and Refine:

Once animations are implemented in the design, designers should iterate and refine animations based on user feedback and observations. Usability testing helps identify areas for improvement and allows designers to iterate on animations iteratively. By gathering feedback from users and observing how they interact with animations, designers can refine animations to ensure they enhance rather than hinder user experience.

5. Optimize for Performance:

Performance optimization is crucial for ensuring smooth and responsive animations across different devices and platforms. Designers should optimize animations for performance by minimizing computational overhead, reducing animation complexity, and leveraging hardware acceleration where available. By prioritizing performance, designers can create animations that enhance user experience without compromising performance.

6. Document Animation Guidelines:

Documenting animation guidelines helps ensure consistency and coherence across different animations within a user interface. Animation guidelines should outline rules and principles for using animation, including specifications for timing, easing curves, and visual styles. By documenting animation guidelines, designers can maintain consistency and coherence in animations, creating a unified perspective and harmonious user experience.

In conclusion, implementing UI animation in design requires careful planning, execution, and iteration. By defining animation goals, storyboarding animations, choosing the right tools, iterating and refining animations, optimizing for performance, and documenting animation guidelines, designers can create animations that enhance usability, engagement, and overall user experience. As technology continues to evolve, the role of UI animation in design will only grow, offering new opportunities for designers to innovate and create compelling digital experiences.

Challenges and Considerations

Implementing UI animation in design comes with its set of challenges and considerations that designers must address to ensure successful execution and optimal user experience. One challenge is striking the right balance between animation and usability. While animation can enhance user engagement and aesthetics, excessive or poorly executed animation can hinder usability and distract users from their tasks. Designers must carefully consider the purpose and context of animations to ensure they add value to the user experience without overwhelming or frustrating users.

Another consideration is performance optimization. Animations can impact the performance of a digital product, particularly on low-powered devices or slow internet connections. Designers must optimize animations for performance by minimizing computational overhead, reducing animation complexity, and leveraging hardware acceleration where available. Prioritizing performance ensures that animations are smooth and responsive across different devices and platforms, enhancing overall user experience.

Accessibility is also a crucial consideration when implementing UI animation. Some users may have disabilities or impairments that affect their ability to perceive or interact with animations. Designers must ensure that animations are accessible to all users by providing alternative means of interaction and avoiding reliance on visual cues alone. Accessibility considerations include factors such as motion sensitivity, cognitive impairments, and screen reader compatibility, which must be taken into account during the design process.

Moreover, maintaining consistency and coherence across animations within a user interface presents another challenge. Inconsistent animation styles, timing, or visual effects can disrupt the flow of the user experience and create confusion for users. Designers must document animation guidelines that outline rules and principles for using animation, including specifications for timing, easing curves, and visual styles. By adhering to animation guidelines, designers can ensure that animations are consistent and coherent, contributing to a unified and harmonious user experience.

In conclusion, while UI animation offers numerous benefits for enhancing user experience and engagement, designers must navigate various challenges and considerations to implement animations effectively. By striking the right balance between animation and usability, optimizing animations for performance, ensuring accessibility, and maintaining consistency and coherence, designers can create animations that enrich the user experience and contribute to the success of digital products and services.

Providing alternative means of interaction and avoiding reliance on visual cues alone. Accessibility considerations include factors such as motion sensitivity, cognitive impairments, and screen reader compatibility, which must be taken into account during the design process.

Interactive Exercises

To reinforce learning, consider the following interactive exercises:

1. **Storyboarding:**

   Practice creating storyboards for different UI animation scenarios, such as transitions between screens or feedback animations for user interactions.

2. **Prototyping:**

   Use prototyping tools to create interactive prototypes that simulate UI animations and test them with users to gather feedback and iterate on designs.

3. **Observation:**

   Observe UI animations in existing digital products and analyze their effectiveness in enhancing engagement and usability.

These exercises will help you apply the concepts learned in this chapter and deepen your understanding of UI animation techniques.

CHAPTER EIGHT
Testing and Feedback

> **"**
>
> Design is where science and art break even.

Testing and feedback play a crucial role in the successful implementation of UI animation in digital design. Through rigorous testing and gathering feedback from users, designers can identify areas for improvement, refine animations, and ensure that they contribute positively to the overall user experience. This section explores various testing methodologies and feedback mechanisms that designers can employ to enhance UI animation implementation.

1. Usability Testing:

Usability testing involves observing users as they interact with animations within the interface and gathering feedback on their experience. Usability testing allows designers to identify usability issues, gauge user satisfaction, and understand how animations impact user behavior. By conducting usability testing, designers can validate design decisions, identify areas for improvement, and iteratively refine animations based on user feedback.

2. A/B Testing:

A/B testing involves comparing two or more versions of an interface with different animations to determine which version performs better in terms of user engagement, conversion rates, or other key metrics. A/B testing allows designers to experiment with different.

3. Prototype Testing:

Prototype testing involves creating interactive prototypes that simulate animations within the interface and testing them with users to gather feedback. Prototype testing allows designers to assess the effectiveness of animations in context and identify any usability issues or pain points. By testing prototypes early in the design process, designers can identify potential problems and make adjustments before finalizing the design.

4. Remote Testing:

Remote testing allows designers to gather feedback from users located in different geographic locations without the need for face-to-face interaction. Remote testing can be conducted through online surveys, remote usability testing platforms, or video conferencing tools. By conducting remote testing, designers can reach a broader audience, gather diverse perspectives, and obtain valuable feedback on animations from users around the world.

5. Feedback Surveys:

Feedback surveys allow designers to gather qualitative feedback from users about their experience with animations within the interface. Surveys can include open-ended questions about users' likes, dislikes, and suggestions for improvement regarding animations. By analyzing survey responses, designers can gain insights into user preferences, pain points, and areas for improvement, informing future design iterations.

6. Expert Reviews:

Expert reviews involve soliciting feedback from usability experts or experienced designers who evaluate animations within the interface based on established usability principles and best practices. Expert reviews can provide valuable insights into the effectiveness of animations in achieving design goals, as well as identify any usability issues or areas for improvement. By incorporating feedback from experts, designers can refine animations and ensure they align with best practices in UI design.

7. Contextual Inquiry:

Contextual inquiry involves observing users in their natural environment as they interact with animations within the interface and gathering insights into their behavior, preferences, and needs. Contextual inquiry allows designers to understand the context in which users interact with animations and identify any usability issues or pain points that may arise. By conducting contextual inquiries, designers can gain valuable insights into user behavior and make informed decisions about how to optimize animations for maximum usability.

8. Analytics Data Analysis:

Analytics data provides quantitative insights into how users interact with animations within the interface, including metrics such as engagement time, interaction frequency, and conversion rates. By analyzing analytics data, designers can identify patterns, trends, and areas for improvement regarding animations. By leveraging analytics data, designers can make data-driven decisions about how to optimize animations to better meet user needs and achieve design goals.

9. Continuous Iteration:

Iteration is key to the successful implementation of UI animation, as it allows designers to refine animations based on user feedback and testing results. Designers should adopt a continuous iteration approach, making incremental improvements to animations over time based on user feedback and observations. By iterating on animations, designers can address usability issues, enhance user engagement, and ensure that animations contribute positively to the overall user experience.

10. Cross-Functional Collaboration:

Collaboration between designers, developers, and other stakeholders is essential for the successful implementation of UI animation. Designers should work closely with developers to ensure that animations are implemented accurately and efficiently within the interface. Collaboration fosters communication, alignment, and mutual understanding between team members, leading to more cohesive and effective animation implementation.

11. User-Centric Design:

User-centric design principles should guide the implementation of UI animation, ensuring that animations are designed with the user's needs, preferences, and expectations in mind. Designers should prioritize usability, accessibility, and inclusivity when designing animations, ensuring that they enhance rather than hinder user experience. By adopting a user-centric design approach, designers can create animations that resonate with users and contribute positively to the overall user experience.

12. Feedback Integration:

Feedback gathered from testing and user feedback mechanisms should be integrated into the design process to inform decision-making and drive continuous improvement. Designers should actively seek feedback from users throughout the design process and use it to iteratively refine animations and optimize user experience. By incorporating feedback into the design process, designers can ensure that animations meet user needs and expectations and achieve design goals effectively.

In conclusion, testing and feedback are essential components of UI animation implementation, helping designers identify usability issues, gather insights into user behavior, and refine animations iteratively. By employing a variety of testing methodologies and feedback mechanisms, designers can ensure that animations contribute positively to the overall user experience and help achieve design goals effectively. Continuous iteration, cross-functional collaboration, user-centric design, and feedback integration are key principles that guide the successful implementation of UI animation and drive continuous improvement in digital design.

CHAPTER NINE

Tools and Resources for UI Designers

"

The details are not the details. They make the design

In the fast-paced world of UI design, having access to the right tools and resources can make all the difference in creating stunning, user-friendly interfaces. From prototyping to collaboration, there's a plethora of tools available to streamline the design process and bring your vision to life. In this section, we'll explore a variety of tools and resources that UI designers can leverage to enhance their workflow and produce exceptional designs.

1. Prototyping Tools:

Prototyping tools allow designers to create interactive prototypes of their designs, enabling them to simulate user interactions and test usability. Popular prototyping tools include Adobe XD, Figma, Sketch, and InVision. These tools offer features such as drag-and-drop interface design, animation capabilities, and real-time collaboration, making it easy for designers to iterate on their designs and gather feedback from stakeholders.

2. Graphic Design Software:

Graphic design software is essential for creating visual assets such as icons, illustrations, and UI elements. Adobe Photoshop, Illustrator, and Affinity Designer are widely used graphic design tools that offer robust features for creating and editing graphics.

3. Wireframing Tools:

Wireframing tools enable designers to create low-fidelity sketches or wireframes of their interface designs, helping them to quickly explore layout ideas and establish the structure of their designs. Balsamiq, Axure RP, and Wireframe.cc are popular wireframing tools that offer intuitive interfaces and drag-and-drop functionality for creating wireframes. These tools allow designers to iterate on their designs rapidly and communicate their ideas effectively to stakeholders.

4. Collaboration Platforms:

Collaboration platforms facilitate communication and collaboration between team members, allowing designers to work together seamlessly on design projects. Slack, Microsoft Teams, and Zoom are commonly used collaboration platforms that offer features such as chat, video conferencing, and file sharing. These platforms enable designers to share ideas, provide feedback, and collaborate in real-time, regardless of geographical location.

5. UI Kits and Templates:

UI kits and templates provide designers with pre-designed elements and layouts that they can use as building blocks for their designs. Websites such as UI8, Creative Market, and Envato Elements offer a wide range of UI kits and templates for various design platforms, including Sketch, Figma, and Adobe XD. These resources save designers time and effort by providing ready-made components that they can customize and integrate into their designs.

6. Typography Resources:

Typography resources provide designers with access to a vast library of fonts, typefaces, and typographic inspiration for their designs. Websites such as Google Fonts, Adobe Fonts, and Typewolf offer extensive collections of web fonts and typographic resources that designers can use to enhance the readability and visual appeal of their designs. These resources

provide designers with valuable insights into typography trends and best practices, helping them choose the right fonts for their projects.

7. Icon Libraries:

Icon libraries offer designers a wide selection of icons and symbols that they can use to enhance the visual hierarchy and usability of their interfaces. Font Awesome, Material Icons, and Flaticon are popular icon libraries that provide thousands of free and premium icons in various styles and formats. These libraries make it easy for designers to find the perfect icons for their designs and customize them to suit their needs.

8. Animation Tools:

Animation tools enable designers to create dynamic and engaging animations for their interfaces, enhancing user experience and visual appeal. Adobe After Effects, Principle, and Lottie are powerful animation tools that offer features such as timeline-based animation editing, motion graphics, and support for exporting animations in web-friendly formats. These tools empower designers to bring their designs to life with fluid animations and interactive transitions.

9. User Testing Platforms:

User testing platforms allow designers to gather feedback from real users about their designs, helping them identify usability issues and make data-driven design decisions. UserTesting, UsabilityHub, and Maze are popular user testing platforms that offer features such as remote usability testing, heatmaps, and analytics. These platforms provide designers with valuable insights into user behavior and preferences, enabling them to optimize their designs for maximum usability and effectiveness.

10. Accessibility Checkers:

Accessibility checkers help designers ensure that their designs are accessible to users with disabilities or impairments, allowing them to identify and fix accessibility issues early in the design process. Axe, WAVE, and Color Contrast Checker are widely used accessibility checkers that offer features such as automated accessibility testing, visual feedback, and recommendations for improvement. These tools help designers create inclusive designs that can be enjoyed by users of all abilities.

11. Version Control Systems:

Version control systems (VCS) enable designers to track changes to their design files, collaborate with team members, and manage project versions effectively. Git, GitHub, and Bitbucket are popular VCS platforms that offer features such as branching, merging, and code review. These platforms provide designers with a centralized repository for their design files, ensuring that changes are tracked and documented throughout the design process.

12. Design Communities and Forums:

Design communities and forums provide designers with opportunities to connect with peers, share knowledge, and seek advice on design-related topics. Websites such as Dribbble, Behance, and Designer Hangout are vibrant design communities where designers can showcase their work, participate in discussions, and gain inspiration from others. These communities foster creativity, collaboration, and professional growth, empowering designers to learn from each other and stay updated on the latest design trends and techniques

13. Online Courses and Tutorials:

Online courses and tutorials offer designers the opportunity to learn new skills and enhance their knowledge of UI design principles and techniques. Platforms such as Udemy, Coursera, and Skillshare offer a wide range of courses on topics such as user interface design, interaction design, and animation. These courses provide designers with structured learning paths, hands-on projects, and expert guidance, helping them develop their skills and advance their careers in UI design.

In conclusion, the right tools and resources can significantly enhance the workflow and productivity of UI designers, enabling them to create exceptional designs that meet user needs and exceed expectations. Whether it's prototyping, collaboration, typography, or animation, there's a tool or resource available to help designers bring their ideas to life and create memorable user experiences. By leveraging these tools and resources effectively, designers can stay ahead of the curve and deliver designs that captivate and inspire users.

CONCLUSION

> **❝**
>
> Great design is a multi-layered relationship between human
> life and its environment

As we draw the curtains on our exploration of intuitive UI design, it's imperative to reflect on the key concepts that have shaped our journey. Throughout this book, we've delved into the intricacies of UI design, unraveling the art and science behind creating interfaces that seamlessly connect users with digital experiences. From understanding user needs to mastering the fundamentals of design and embracing cutting-edge techniques, our quest for intuitive interfaces has been nothing short of enlightening.

At the heart of intuitive UI design lies a deep-rooted commitment to user-centricity. By placing users at the forefront of the design process, we empower ourselves to craft experiences that resonate deeply with their needs, preferences, and behaviors. Through empathy and insight, we gain a profound understanding of the human psyche, allowing us to anticipate their desires and deliver solutions that exceed their expectations.

Throughout our exploration, we've encountered numerous principles and best practices that underpin intuitive UI design. From the importance of visual hierarchy and typography to the nuances of color theory and animation each element plays a vital role in shaping user experiences. By embracing these principles and leveraging them in our designs, we create interfaces that not only delight the senses but also guide users seamlessly through their digital journey.

As we reflect on our journey, it's clear that intuitive UI design is more than just a technical skill—it's an art form. It requires creativity, empathy, and a relentless pursuit of excellence. It's about distilling complexity into simplicity, transforming chaos into order, and imbuing every interaction with purpose and meaning. It's a continuous process of refinement and iteration, fueled by curiosity and a relentless desire to push the boundaries of what's possible.

In the grand tapestry of digital design, intuitive interfaces stand as beacons of innovation and empathy, guiding users through the vast expanse of the digital landscape with grace and ease. They are the embodiment of our commitment to excellence, our dedication to craftsmanship, and our unwavering belief in the transformative power of design. As we bid farewell to these pages, let us carry forth the lessons learned and the insights gained, continuing our quest to craft experiences that enrich the lives of users around the world.

In closing, let us remember that intuitive UI design is not merely a destination but a journey—a journey marked by discovery, experimentation, and growth. It's a journey that invites us to push beyond our comfort zones, challenge the status quo, and

dare to dream of a future where technology serves humanity in ways we never thought possible. So let us embrace this journey with open hearts and open minds, knowing that with each step we take, we inch closer to a world where intuitive interfaces reign supreme, and digital experiences transcend the ordinary to become truly extraordinary.

As we part ways, I leave you with this thought: the path to intuitive UI design is paved with curiosity, empathy, and a relentless commitment to excellence. So go forth, dear reader, and let your designs be a testament to the boundless potential of human creativity and ingenuity. For in the world of UI design, the possibilities are endless, and the journey is yours to chart. Bon voyage!

Copyright Notice